MW00331757

Making your own Pâté

Joyce van Doorn

Making your own Pâté

Make your own chicken liver pâté, jugged hare pâté, salmon mousse, mushroom pâté, sausagemeat bread, steak-and-kidney pie, fish pâté, or vegetable pâté.

Prism Press, Great Britain   Chronicle Books, USA

Published 1980 in Great Britain by
PRISM PRESS
Stable Court
Chalmington
Dorchester, Dorset DT2 0HB

and in the USA by
Chronicle Books
870 Market Street
Suite 915
San Francisco
CA 94102

Originally published in Holland by Uitgeverij Bert Bakker 1979

Translated by Andy and Nicolette Colborne in association with First Edition

Illustrations by Jane Greenwood

ISBN 0 907061 01 X Hardback (U.K.)
ISBN 0 907061 02 8 Paperback (U.K.)

Printed in Great Britain by
The Garden City Press Ltd., Letchworth, Herts.

Contents

Introduction

My first acquaintance with pâté was some 30 years ago when, soon after the war, my French grandmother re-introduced the tradition of the New Year dinner for the whole family. This dinner always started with *pâté de foie gras de Strasbourg*, which was served on a bed of lettuce on a silver plate and surrounded by crisp sour gherkins, olives, strips of red pepper, and accompanied by warm toast. We children really enjoyed this, although the culinary nuances were lost on us. We thought that truffles, so highly praised by connoisseurs, were awful and we would deposit them on the plates of the grown-ups. But we used to cover many a piece of toast with pâté and would sample the rest of the meal just to be polite. Our appetite would return in time for the dessert.

Later, during travels through France, my appreciation broadened and I learnt to enjoy *pâté de campagne, terrine de la maison* and fish pâté. Very often our picnic lunch consisted of a piece of pâté (bought at a local delicatessen and having a different flavour each time), with fresh French bread, a little French cheese and a glass of red wine. We would do justice to this in a quiet wood with the smell of pine needles and the rustling of leaves above our heads, inviting us to a siesta.

Your first introduction to pâté is like a first love, you never forget it. One of the most beautiful songs in praise of pâté (though not fully endorsed by me) is by the Rev. Sydney Smith, a frivolous vicar from Victorian times: '. . . my idea of heaven is eating pâté de foie gras to the sound of trumpets.' Personally I would prefer a gipsy string-band, but in the old days trumpets were favoured. They were a sign of triumph and of royal honour; Elizabeth I of England, for instance, would enhance her dinners and banquets with the sound of trumpets.

Via a simple chicken liver pâté I started down the slippery path of pâté making, but it did not turn out to be half as slippery as I had always thought. Now, not only do I make pâté for special occasions or when I am expecting guests, but also when I feel like giving myself a treat. Usually, when I prepare a dish that has to be eaten immediately, I lose my appetite by the time it is ready; and that's just as well in this case because most pâtés and terrines have to be left in the refrigerator for a few days after preparation.

Another advantage of the standing time (for instance, in the case of a large dinner party) is that I do not have to prepare everything at the last minute, and can devote all my time to the other dishes without having to worry about the first course. Pâté is good at almost any time of the day; and something to keep in the house for unexpected visits. Pâté offers countless possibilities. Apart from recipes for chicken liver pâtés, vol-au-vents and pâté de foie gras, this book also contains recipes for pâté maison, terrines, gelatines, fish cakes, fish puddings, mousses, pies, quiches, potted meat and vegetarian pâtés. All these closely related recipes are described in the next chapter.

What is pâté?

Take some meat, fish, poultry, game and/or liver, cut or mince it and mix with fat and spices, put it in a small dish lined with pastry or bacon, cook it slowly in the oven, and 'then it is perfect'—so said Thomas van der Noot of his 'Pâté' in *Een notabel boecxken van cokereyen* from about 1510 (a distinguished cookery book).

Pâté is as simple as that. But it does not have to be so simple; you can make it as complicated as you like. Variations on the pâté theme are endless and range from a simple Dutch liver pâté to an adventurous terrine of pheasant with herbs and cognac.

Almost all over the world pâté is eaten in one form or another; apparently, pastry and filling are a natural combination. In England, there are pies and pasties; in Spain, pastel and empañadas; in Italy, pasticcio and ravioli; in East Europe, pirog, kromeski, serniki and pirajki. The Chinese, Japanese, Arabs, Iranians and Hindustanis also know the delicacies of pastry with savoury fillings.

The French, from whom the word *'pâté'* comes, describe it as follows: 'A pastry (pâte) which covers meat, filling (farce) or fish, all cooked together. Pâtés can be divided into two categories: warm and cold pâtés; they can be baked in a tin (pâtés en croûte) or put in a terrine, and their shapes are very variable.' (Taken from '*Larousse ménagère*'). A multiplicity of words like pâte, pâté, pastete, pastry, pie, pastei, patty, pasticcio, pastel and others taken from the Latin '*pasta*') mean exactly the same as the French word '*pâté*'. Nowadays, the notion of 'pastei' is largely restricted to a case of puff pastry filled with a ragout of some sort, but here and there it is beginning to regain its original, broader meaning.

What in English is called pâté, the French call *terrine*. A terrine is a pâté without a pastry crust, but which is covered instead by a small layer of fat so that it keeps for longer. In France, too, the difference between pâté and terrine is slowly disappearing and the words are interchangeable. Terrine is named after the container in which it is cooked, originally an earthenware *terra* = earth) bowl with a lid. Terrines were also made of cast iron, mostly enamelled, and of porcelain and recently of ovenproof glass. There are the most beautiful antique forms ingeniously modelled with curls and scrolls, and some very simple rustic ones.

The English version of *pâté en croûte* (in a crust) is the *raised pie*. The pie is a sort of flat tart, sweet or savoury, which usually still has its pastry lid left. This contrasts with a quiche which has lost its lid. In the last century, an open flan with a basic filling of cream and eggs was called a *kiche*. A pie has a number of different meanings for the British. Some-times, the pastry lid is replaced by a layer of mashed potato, or by some sort of batter. A *'tureen'* is the French terrine, and *patties* are pastries.

A *galantine* has the same ingredients as the pâté or terrine, but is made in a different way. The filling is either put in a bird which has

been boned, or in a skin with a little fat or meat still attached, or sewn in a thin slice of meat. The whole thing is then tied in a napkin, hung in stock and cooked. A galantine is usually served cold, surrounded by a little jelly. Pâtés often used to consist of boned, stuffed birds, cooked in a crust, and that is how the galantine originated. Sometimes a large bird was used which would be filled with progressively smaller birds and the gaps would be filled with minced meat.

The *pudding* originated in England and, like the galantine, was hung in stock to cook or steam. In former times, this was done in the stomachs of certain animals; nowadays it is usually tied up in a pudding bag or napkin.

In this book, a *mousse* is a light savoury pudding (this is the Dutch meaning which has, slowly but surely, become applicable in England too) prepared with stiffly beaten egg white or whipping cream.

Potted meat, confits and *rillettes* are all very much alike. All three are made of potted meat, poultry or game, with spices, covered with a thin layer of fat, and usually kept in glass preserving jars.

Not only can you use meat, fish, poultry, game and liver for pâté, but also vegetables, beans, mushrooms, eggs, cream and cheese, or a combination of these, to prepare a delicious filling. What would you think of a fish pâté with a layer of sorrel, spinach or nettles, or a beef and kidney pâté with oysters, a cabbage pâté with mushrooms, or a Danish liver pâté with anchovies?

Starting from a basic mixture of your choice, you can vary your pâté by adding different spices, by mixing in some drink or by adding different kinds of nuts, olives, tropical fruits, etc., either chopped up or in coarse pieces. This is what gives your pâté the personal touch which you don't get when you buy pâté from your butcher or delicatessen. This is inevitable because such pâtés are nearly all factory-made. Confectioners who used to make their own special pâtés disappeared over 100 years ago, very few remain who sell their own home-made suet rolls, pastries and crusts for vol-au-vents (the latter are also classed as pâtés).

So, to present something special on the meal table, we must set to work ourselves. Really and truly, pâté-making is a challenge—a culinary adventure.

The History of Pastries & Pâté

Through the ages, feasts and banquets have been graced with pastries. They were, and still are, the showpieces on which chefs can unleash their artistic and culinary talents. Pastries were the pride of the host and hostess. Often the blazon (coat of arms) was paraded on the table, sculptured in dough and filled with all sorts of delicacies. Strongholds and castles were built; a duck would be modelled in dough around a stuffed chicken and the most fantastic scenes would be depicted.

Fertility symbols decorated the wedding table. In Braunschweig, for example, it was customary until after 1600 to serve a so-called 'Brautburg' at weddings. This consisted of a castle made from dough with a roasted cock and four living birds inside and on top a large phallic symbol, decorated with ribbons (Bänder). However, the Brautburg was banned in 1608 because of its 'obscene' meaning. German kingdoms had other such regulations to militate against offensive pastry exhibitions.

Pastry cooks

Not only the rich and their guests enjoyed pastries; the less well-off used to tuck into them too, though in a simpler form. And they did not have to cook them for themselves as pastry cooks existed even then.

Johannes de Garlandia, an Englishman who lived mainly in Paris and died in 1252, wrote that pastry cooks earned a lot of money and that 'they sell to everyone pork and poultry pastries and lamprey pastries with pepper (very special in those days) and they display cakes and flans made with soft cheese and fresh eggs . . .'. Chaucer tells too, in his 14th century *Canterbury Tales* of pastry vendors in London.

For centuries the citizens of London could go to Pye Corner, where pastry cooks sold portions of pie from the oven, hot or cold. Pastry baking was mainly done by men, except in the kitchens of the lower classes, who could not afford a cook and had only a kitchenmaid. The Ancient Egyptians were an exception to this rule, as they allowed women in their kitchens to prepare the savoury or sweet pastries. They thought women had a gift for this sort of work.

Many good chefs started as apprentices to pastry cooks. The most famous example is the Frenchman Antoine Carème. His *'pièces montées'* were famous all over Europe. His apprentice, Jules Gouffé, praises the trade of pâtissier and says in the foreword of his *'Livre de pâtisserie'* that a good pastry baker can become an excellent cook but not vice versa. He can even become a great *'rôtisseur'* (somebody who roasts meat). This opinion is contradicted by Brillat-Savarin, famous gourmet and writer on the pleasures of dining: *'On devient cuisinier, mais on naît rôtisseur'* (one becomes a cook but one is born a 'rôtisseur'). According to Gouffé, cooking is not so much a gift of birth but more a question of timing.

The Romans

The principle of pastry-making is as old as the road to Rome, and we can safely assume that it is even older. In any case, the Romans were familiar with vegetable, meat and fruit pastries. Apart from enjoying pastries, the Romans used them to play practical jokes on their guests. The story goes that at a dinner given by a certain Trimalchio, a new dish was brought in at a chosen moment, which to everybody's disappointment contained only a wooden hen. The hen was sitting on eggs and

Trimalchio invited his guests to smash the eggs with their spoons to see if they were fertilised. The eggs were really made of dough, but the guests thought they saw embryos in the egg yolks and, horrified, wanted to throw them away. On closer inspection the embryo was seen to be a well-done fig-eater (a small bird), so the guests ate up their eggs after all.

Fooling guests was a sport. Apicio, for example, in his *'De re coquinaria'*, the oldest known cookery book, included a recipe for serving up a fish made of meat as well as a number of recipes for pastries.

Pastries were also renowned for their flavour and this is shown by a saying of Emperor Claudius. Once, during a court hearing, he sat deep in thought and gazing into space. He let everybody rant and rave, then suddenly stood up and interrupted the speakers with the words: 'Meat pastries are delicious. We shall have them for dinner'.

The Middle Ages and the Renaissance

We learn from Garlandia that pastries already existed in the early Middle Ages. They were probably one of the many things left behind by the Romans who certainly had an influence on the art of cooking, in spite of the opposition of the Christian Fathers to everything Roman, especially the extravagant ways that these 'decadent' rulers introduced. But the very fact that there was so much preaching against it is an indication that many Roman customs had already been adopted and that people were reluctant to give up these luxuries, once they had sampled them. In the time of William the Conqueror (11th century) the English had a rather sinister name for the pastries in which a small bird or a whole fruit was cooked in a pastry crust: they called them 'cofyns', or coffins. This pastry crust was very hard, and was not meant to be eaten. A pastry crust that could be eaten was called 'fayre paste'.

The Middle Ages and the Renaissance were the renowned periods of pastry making. Pastries were baked not so much for their contents, but more for decoration or as a joke. In the Middle Ages, people had in fact the same predilections and sense of humour as the Romans, and they even went a step further sometimes. The recipe for a goose, roasted alive, given in both the 16th century book by the English doctor Wecker, and that by the Neapolitan naturalist Porta, is really cruel and repulsive. Both books were read all over Europe, and were reprinted many times, but one hopes this bears witness to curiosity rather than to the actual practice of the recipe.

Giambattista Porta tells something of the history of the recipe in his 'Magia naturalis'. Such a suffering animal is said to have been served more than once on the King of Arragon's table, not long before Porta was born. Finally, out of curiosity, and to see if it really was possible, Porta carried out the experiment himself. His guests were so impatient that the animal was eaten before it was completely done, and he noted that the animal was still alive, and was best roasted on the outside of the crust.

Living creatures in pastry

Baking living creatures in pastry became a highly-prized art which was described in many cookery books of the Middle Ages and the Renaissance. In Rijssel, in 1454, people went so far as to hide a complete orchestra in an enormous pastry, which started playing when the showpiece was cut open. Orchestras in those days were not as large as they are now, however, and you should certainly not imagine that the pastry contained a complete symphony orchestra. It was more likely to have been a small string band of about 6 people.

Frantz de Rontzier had somewhat simpler ideas in his *Kunstbuch von mancherley Essen, Gesotten, Posteten, von Hirschen, Vogelen, Wildprat und andern Schawessen* from 1598. Apart from some 180 recipes for pastries he gives the following recipe: 'Clean a living cock, (or small bird, or partridge), decorate its neck, beak, and legs, hang small bells around its neck and legs; place it between 2 deep dishes, and when the womenfolk are seated at long tables, carry these dishes to them, and open them up immediately.' Eels between two dishes also worked well according to De Rontzier, but still better was to put them in a roasted pig, 'so that the eels wriggle over the table! and that is a fine feast for the womenfolk!'

SING A SONG OF SIXPENCE

Sing a song of sixpence, A pocket full of rye Four and twenty blackbirds baked in a pie

When the pie was opened the birds began to sing, Wasn't that a dainty dish to set before the King

For fun, living lobsters were coloured red with brandy, and put between cooked lobsters. Rontzier does not mention what you should do if a finger got trapped between the pincers.

England

The English learnt the skill of concealing living creatures in pastry from an Italian, Epulario. His cookery book was translated into English in 1598 and was the first to have a recipe for living birds in pastry. Birds provided all manner of table joys. If singing birds were used they warbled when the pie was opened. Some birds would fly to the light and extinguish the candles with their flapping wings, which allowed cats to grab them in the dark.

Other birds served as prey for the falcons of gentlemen. This was an exciting pastime which gave rise to betting, and the bloodbath that followed would increase the appetite of the guests. Sometimes the birds (caught by using twigs smeared with bird-lime) would quickly be taken to the kitchen in order to be prepared for the next course. Singing birds are the theme of an English nursery rhyme which must have originated from that time:

> Sing a song of sixpence, a pocket full of rye
> Four-and-twenty blackbirds baked in a pie
> When the pie was opened the birds began
>   to sing
> Oh, wasn't that a dainty dish to set before a
>   King.

The King in question was probably Charles I, whose master chef published a book in 1664, *The Accomplished Chef*, about a style of cooking which at that time must have already been out of fashion. This chef, Robert May, described the recipes with which he delighted the English-Scottish Court in the first half of the 17th century: 'live frogs leaping from a pie will make the ladies jump and scream, to the amusement of the whole company', so he says. Even the King's dwarf had to suffer and was dressed up as a warrior, put inside a pie and thus introduced to the Queen.

The height of beauty was surely reached in the house of Lord Nevill, trustee of Elizabeth I of England, a well-known Lucullian. He, or his cook, must have been a refined man for those days. During a grand party given by Lord Nevill, a giant pie was carried in from which, when the crust was cut open, hundreds of butterflies rose out and remained fluttering about in the hall. This period of extravagant pastries, which incidentally were formally restricted to the Court, came to an end in England halfway through the 17th century, not only because of high costs, but also because the church protested against the excesses. When the Great Fire of London started in Pudding Lane in 1666, Puritans regarded this as an expression of God's wrath directed against the gourmets and gastronomes. This street was so named by Elizabeth I because she adored puddings and pastries. (The savoury pudding of those times would nowadays be called a terrine or galantine.)

France

The French court did not acquire a refined kitchen until after the arrival of Catherine de Medici and her Italian chefs in 1533 and was not familiar with any of the unusual pastries known to the English court. The edible contents were probably of more importance to the French. As far as the shape of the pie was concerned they did not go beyond the usual castles and fortresses complete with towers, ramparts, stockades, and drawbridges. For something out of the ordinary, small cannons which could be fired would sometimes be placed on the ramparts.

At the table of the Sun King, Louis XIV, many warm pastries were served with the first and second courses like the 'Pasté' of boned and stuffed capon, with musk, and the 'pasté Roi Soleil' with young pigeons on a bed of tender green peas. A famous book from those days was 'Le Pâstissier françois' printed in 1655 in Amsterdam by the Elsevier brothers. The most important part of this book is filled with recipes for savoury pastries, 'pastés' as the French called them at the time.

Ordinary pastries and pâtès were often eaten by the French. A Venetian Ambassador to the French Court in the 16th century reported how surprised he was to find a pâtisserie in every town and village on his way through France. Not only could one buy hot and cold ready-cooked pastries, but also uncooked ones to take away and bake at home. The custom has survived to this day in Italy and France, except that in France it has now been replaced by the charcuterie and in Italy by the salumeria.

The Netherlands

The Low Countries were a little more restrained in their pastry designs, but until the 18th century pastries frequently appeared on the meal-table. It was a welcome change from the bread and parsnips usually eaten with meat. The Dutch did not become potato-eaters until the end of the 18th century. Until the 19th century many a pastry recipe could be found in Dutch cookery books, and usually a separate chapter was devoted to these, together with the 'toerten' (tarts) and 'podd-ingen' (puddings) which were often savoury.

In this book, Thomas van der Noot followed up a few general recipes with a whole series of unusual recipes for 'pasteyen' (pastries):

'How to make good pastry. Take some flour, and make a dough with it, adding eggs or lard, because the pastry crust should be short. Then take whatever meat you wish to put in it, and chop it up accordingly. Or take capons or hens, or cows' tongues or game, and put them in the pastry. And the game should be larded with cloves. Some people add chopped-up bacon. The herbs to use are ginger, cardamom and cinnamon, mixed together. These spices should be rubbed into the chopped meat, and all this should be put in the pastry. A little wine can be added if you wish. One also adds bone marrow as it should be greasy. Put it in the oven and let it cook. Then it is perfect.'

At the end of the chapter on pastries in *Een notabel boecxken van cokereyen*, (a dist-inguished cookery book from 1510) is a recipe for a meat pie which finishes with the words: 'And you should let it cook like a pastry, but the top should be open, like other kinds of tarts'. This clearly explains the difference between pastries and tarts. In the 18th century a new type of pastry appeared, the 'papiton', adapted from the French cuisine, *'poulpeton'* or *'poupeton'*. The *'Nieuwe Vaderlandsche Kookkunst'* (The New National Art of Cooking) of 1794, written by two very experienced housekeepers, contains recipes for all sorts of ordinary (to us) pastries (except for the stork pie), 'puddings' and tarts—and also papiton.

Papiton of lamb cutlets

Prepare the cutlets as you would for grilling, but make them a little shorter; toss them in flour mixed with salt and breadcrumbs—then fry them in butter until brown and let them cool; prepare a pastry in the same way as for tarts; put in a papiton mould, place the cutlets on top and cover them with the same sort of pastry, close the mould, and leave the meat to cook in the oven until done. Next you prepare a coulée of fried flour with the juice of shallots, leave this to simmer for a while, rub it through a sieve, add a few morellos, (some people also add a few pieces of sweetbread), a few spices, lemon juice, some pepper, and salt to taste. When the papiton is done, you take off the top, add the prepared coulée and serve.'

The English also copied this recipe from the French, and called it a 'pupton'. The following is a 'Pupton of Pigeon'.

Make a well-greased mixture of veal or chicken, fatty bacon, suet, mushrooms, spinach, parsley, thyme, marjoram, savory, and onions into a pastry and line a dish with it. Cover this with the thin strips of bacon, pigeon, asparagus tips, mushrooms, hard-boiled egg yolks, cock's comb, and *Pallets*, cover with a layer of the mixture, bake in the oven and serve covered with gravy.

Sometimes sweetbread, sweet potatoes and artichokes were used in the filling.

The changing of recipes

The *poulpeton* was the French version of the Italian *polpettone*, a roll of minced beef wrapped in a slice of meat, which the Dutch now call a *blinde vink* (beef olive). The poulpeton consisted of a ragoût made with minced beef and covered with thin slices of veal. Neither the *papiton* nor the *pupton* bear the slightest resemblance to this. This kind of confusion occurred quite often with recipes: they turned up everywhere and seemed to have a life of their own. Changes came about when an author interpreted a foreign recipe, or by the chef's imagination, or by the addition of ingredients which were to hand.

Europeans have travelled a lot since Roman times, no matter how difficult it was at the time. As a result of foreign rule, wars, crusades, and more especially pilgrimages, people became familiar with exotic dishes and preparation methods. Later, this knowledge was broadened by commerce and exploration. The *Ménagier de Paris*, a housekeeping book written by an affluent senior citizen of Paris for his ignorant and very young wife to help her in the running of a fairly large household, gave the recipe for a Lombardy pie and a Norwegian pie made of minced fresh liver.

Not many French recipes could be found in other countries before the 17th century. The only cookery books that contained a recipe for French pastry were Anna Wecker's cookery book of 1597 and de Rontzier's of 1598. Until that time, Italian and Spanish recipes were favourites in European cuisine, which was fairly international.

England after the 18th century

Only for a short time did the Puritans in England succeed in curbing the extravagant dinners given by the nobility and the middle classes. The new period of excess which began at the end of the 17th century, was a reaction to their sober life-style. What is more, in the 18th century the English seemed to go through a long bout of *spleen* (depression and boredom), and what better remedy was there for this than food, drink and entertainment.

This again resulted in a hangover—that is, a depression—and so people ended up trapped in a vicious circle behaving more and more extravagantly.

People became more Roman than the Romans, except in their eating habits which were medieval. Once again all kinds of animals jumped from pies, fountains spurted wine and Lord Albemarle's chef made such an enormous tower of gods and goddesses that the structure would not fit into the dining-hall. 'Can you imagine?', complained the *confiseur*, 'milord would not even remove the ceiling!'

Once again, geese or ducks were plucked alive, surrounded by apple sauce (to quench the thirst of the animal) put in a ring of fire and thus roasted alive. The English recipe, described by Doctor William Kitchener ends with the words: '. . . she will cry as you cut off any part from her and will be almost eaten up before she be dead; it is mighty pleasant to behold!'

Cruelty was a means to while away boredom, and all kinds of ways to torture animals were thought up, in order to render the meat more tasty and tender. I shall spare you the details. The poet Alexander Pope (1688-1744) writes about it: 'I know nothing more shocking or horrific than the prospect of kitchens covered in blood and filled with the cries of animals who suffer death by torture.' And die by torture they did.

But let us get back to more pleasant subjects. The demand in those days was for size and quantity, and so the pies assumed gigantic proportions. Everything to be found in a kitchen, apart from utensils, was hidden under a crust. Neither cost nor trouble was spared over Christmas pies, which were proof of the competence of the cook, kitchenmaid or housewife. A certain Mrs Patterson, hostess at Howick in 1744, needed two strong men to carry in her 168 lbs Christmas pie. The pie consisted of 2 bushels of flour, 20 lbs of butter, 4 geese, 2 turkeys, 2 rabbits, 4 wild ducks, 2 woodcocks, 6 snipe, 4 partridges, 2 ox tongues, 7 blackbirds and 6 pigeons.

The eating habits of the English upper classes were greatly influenced by French cuisine. The nobility paid a lot of money for French cooks. Later, at the time of the French Revolution and during the Napoleonic Wars, many cooks escaped to England, not so much because they were afraid for their heads, but because there was no money left to pay for the expensive concoctions. Antoine Carême was not one of them. He actually had to be tempted to come to England by the Prince Regent, later King George IV, but he did not stay long in the Brighton Pavilion. Carême probably felt that an Englishman was not capable of fully appreciating his refined cuisine. Still, the pâtés he created were sold for a lot of money. They were sold from the Prince Regent's dinner table to rich citizens, at the backdoor of the Pavilion still hot. This was fat to the fire of the satirists of that time:

A napkin let my temples bind
in nightgown free and unconfined

And undisturbed by women
All boons of one, I ask of pâté
At city feasts, to eat my weight,
And drink enough to swim in.

The French influence quickly came to an end after George VI, because his successor, William IV, (1830-1837), was a stingy man, who economised on everything. This included food, and he dismissed all French cooks to the court, as a result of which the quality of cooking went down considerably. This prompted Lord Dudley to say: 'What a change to be sure—cold pâté and hot champagne.' Queen Victoria, who succeeded him, was also no connoisseur, but her son, later Edward VII, loved good food. He took it so seriously that his friends nick-named him 'Tum-Tum'. In the 19th century pies and raised pies were found mainly on the tables of peasants and the lower classes. The upper classes preferred to serve a 'pupton', 'tureen', or 'galantine'.

Holland after the 18th century

After the 18th century, pastries were eaten less and less in Holland. Recipes for pastries, pies and pâtés disappeared from the cookery books; the *Nieuwe Burgerkeukenboek* (the New Middle Class cookery book) recorded only five in 1833. Pâtés, pies and pastries were still prepared in the foreign-oriented kitchens of a few well-off citizens, and in restaurants too, France was a fashionable country for a long time (do you remember the French nanny?). Many official menus were drawn up in French, offering French dishes. A good example of this is the menu which Hotel Derlon in Maasttricht offered to its guests on Good Friday for the sum of 1 guilder:

Menu de Diner de Vendredi-Saint 1869

Potage Bordelais
Sardines de Nantes
Petits pâtés chauds
Turbot, sauce Hollandaise
Filets de sole à l'Italienne
Petits-poids à la Française
Brochets aux champignons
Mayonnaise d'anguilles
Buissons de homards
Salade nouvelle
Pudding diplomate
Fruits, Dessert
Glaces
à la Florin le couvert

There is only one pâté on the whole menu.

Nor did confectioners in the 19th century show any interest in pâté. No pastries or pâtés can be found in the professional literature of that time, only vol-au-vents and empty pastry cases. *The Amsterdamsche Banketbakker* (The Amsterdam Confectioner) from 1866 has no savoury recipes at all, apart from one for stock cubes, which looks very odd amongst all the sweet things.

Until halfway through the 20th century hardly any recipes for pâté and pastries could be found in cookery books. In *translated* cookery books, yes, for in other countries pâtés and pies kept their place in everyday kitchens and restaurants. Often recipes were passed on from mother to daughter, and from chef to apprentice. One cannot imagine an English kitchen without a pie, or a French or Belgian kitchen without a pâté.

Happily, the Dutch have renewed their acquaintance with pâté and pastries. Thanks to holidays abroad they have begun to take a place in their kitchens. Many restaurants have pâté and pastries on their menus and in addition to a few specialised cookery books on pâté, many general cookery books now contain a few recipes for various pâtés.

The Right Utensils

The right utensils are half the battle in pâté-making. They save both temper and time: to spend a whole afternoon mincing liver through a blunt mincer isn't much fun.

Below is a list of essential, and not quite so essential, though helpful, kitchen utensils.

Knives

The only truly indispensable item is a good, sharp knife or, even better, a few knives for trimming liver, slicing fatty bacon into strips, making large or small cubes of meat or for chopping up a few herbs. Some people prefer to chop up finely all the meat for a pâté. Less juice is extracted from the meat in this way than when putting it through a mincer: mincers squeeze out the juices. A good knife is expensive, but it lasts a life time. As far as I am concerned, you can economise on all other kitchen utensils, but a knife is worth the investment.

A knife needs a steel to sharpen it, for even the best knife gets blunt eventually, especially if you cut onto something hard, like a plate.

My father used to sharpen two knives on each other—which put my teeth on edge—but I have never managed to do this well and prefer a knife-sharpener.

Anyway, no matter how you do it, a knife should be as sharp as a razor blade. An excellent way to put away knives with sharp ends is to stick corks on them, as is done with fencing foils.

Mincer

The same goes for a mincer as for a knife: the blades should be sharp. You should also be able to fix the mincer firmly, for it will be subjected to hard labour.

There are all kinds of mincers on the market: the old-fashioned but very effective hand-mills, and various electric ones. Should you decide to buy the latter, you would be well-advised to have a good look around first. Or you could, like me, keep borrowing from a neighbour or friend, until you have found the one that suits you best. If you are on very good terms with your butcher, you can ask him to mince the meat or liver for you. He's doing you a big favour if he does, because the machine usually has to be thoroughly cleaned before he can use it again.

However, the advantage of mincing yourself is that you can regulate the coarseness, which affects the nature of the pâté.

A mincer is not necessary for every pâté. Certainly not for a vegetable, cheese or fish pâté, and even chicken livers can quite easily be ground in a drum sieve or in a mortar, if you fry them briefly first.

Chopping board

A wooden chopping board will protect your knives. A large one is handiest because it prevents things from falling off so easily.

Mixing bowl

A few large mixing bowls are nice to have, but large dishes will also do.

A firm wooden ladle and a spatula

Garlic press

Rolling-pin

Baking moulds

Baking moulds are very suitable for pâtés in a pastry crust, provided they are jointless. However, baking moulds are not very elegant for serving, and tin moulds are definitely not advisable for a pâté without a crust. The metal soon gives the meat mixture a tinny taste.

Pie dishes and terrines

Down the centuries many different kinds of pie dishes have been made—simple smooth earthenware, and embossed china. Oval, round and rectangular. With handsome lids in the shape of a duck or pheasant, or a hare's head. High ones and low ones, small ones and large ones. There are cast iron and enamelled pie dishes, which have the advantage that they last a long time and do not develop a stale smell, like earthenware dishes do if they are stored away closed. But the contents are what really matters, and a very simple, fairly deep ovenproof dish does the job very well. Even the lid is not important, as you can cover a pâté with kitchen foil.

Roasting tin

A roasting tin or some pan or dish that your terrine will fit into is necessary to cook the pâté *au-bain-marie*.

Trivet or grid

The earthenware or china ones are the best (like those used for fish and asparagus) for draining pâtés.

Basic Ingredients

Pork

The pig, with its characteristic, full flavour is the most important animal in pâté-making. 'De la tête à la queue, tout est bon,' (from top to bottom, it's all delicious) say the French. Not only the flesh, but nearly all parts of the pig can be used in pâté: the liver, the head and bacon fat for the filling; back bacon, middle bacon and the abdominal and gut walls to line the pie dish; the trotters to make a stock, then allowed to gel for aspic. The prime cuts like ham and fricandeau and kidneys and sweetbread, can be chopped into strips or pieces and layered in the filling.

In many pâtés and terrines minced pork is the basic filling, and in poultry and game pâtés. If you buy minced pork from your butcher, then use slightly less fat in your pâté than indicated. Such mince is usually very fatty, but this of course depends on the butcher. If you mince the meat yourself, then do not use the best cuts. Pork steaks or boned pork cutlets produce the same, if not better results. A little fat on the meat is all right; pâté was originated as a way of using up left-overs.

Veal

Veal, with its milder flavour, is suitable for pâtés and terrines with a soft, delicate flavour. Such a pâté should not be too spicy, otherwise you might as well use pork, which is cheaper. The same applies to minced veal as minced pork.

Beef

Beef is not often used in pâté-making, but it is found in certain pies, like steak and kidney. It seems a pity to use tender cuts (they are better for grilling or frying) and the cuts that are not so nice take too long to cook for a pâté. Lean minced beef, preferably home-minced, is very suitable.

Lamb and mutton

A lamb or mutton pâté or pie is very rare. The meat has a rather pronounced flavour, as has the offal.

Poultry and game

The flesh of all poultry or game is well-suited to pâté, and terrine. The prime parts, like saddle and leg of hare and rabbit, saddle and haunch of venison, and the breasts and legs of game-birds, are not worked into the filling, but are cut into strips or pieces and placed between layers of filling. Sometimes they are marinated first in an alcoholic drink.

The boning of a raw piece of game or poultry can cause problems. If you first fry or boil the meat briefly, boning is a lot easier. Cooked left-overs are very good for pâté and can be supplemented with other ingredients such as chicken livers or pork pieces. So next time you eat game or poultry, start with a little extra and make this into a pâté the following day.

Fish

In principle all kinds of fish can be used for a fish pâté. Anchovy is used in some liver pâtés—a combination of meat and fish that was introduced by the Romans. Now it is usually called Danish.

Liver

Liver is an important ingredient of many pâtés and terrines. Calf's liver has the mildest flavour, pig and ox livers are a bit stronger and lamb and mutton livers are the strongest. Pig and calf livers are the most used. Chicken livers are very often used in pâtés, in spite of their very special flavour. The flavour becomes milder if you soak the livers in milk for about an hour. You can also do this with other strong-tasting livers.

Duck and goose livers are a delicacy, but they are very difficult to get hold of, especially out of season. Goose liver is actually in a class of its own; the enlarged liver, so highly prized by the French, is very difficult to come by elsewhere, but so are the small ones. Perhaps your poulterer can find them for you on a special occasion, especially around Christmas, when people eat more geese.

Bacon

Bacon is an essential ingredient of pâtés. It makes for smoothness: a pâté with too little fat is dry and crumbles quickly. Always use fatty bacon, without rind. Back bacon is somewhat better than middle bacon, but both can be used. Never use smoked bacon, except when you want to produce a very special effect, because it overpowers the other flavours. Fatty belly pork membranes and gut membranes are used mainly by professional pâté-makers for lining terrines. Your butcher can order it for you. Put it in lukewarm water until you start using it, to keep it nice and supple.

Herbs, spices and salt

See next chapter.

Onions, shallots and garlic

An ordinary onion is usually slightly sweeter than a shallot, but shallots are said to be more digestible. That is why they are much used in French cuisine. They blend a bit better into the filling and can be cut more easily into small pieces because of their finer texture. Garlic is very good in pâté. The flavour can be predominant but need not be, depending on your preference. Sometimes you can hardly smell or taste the garlic in a pâté, but you would miss it if it was not there. Together with other herbs and spices, it gives a lovely full aroma.

A very finely chopped garlic clove is milder than one squeezed out in a press.

Eggs, flour, breadcrumbs and rusk crumbs

These are used to bind the forcemeat, just as with meat balls. Breadcrumbs can be fresh or dried. You can make dry crumbs by lightly roasting a few slices of bread in the oven until they are thoroughly dry and golden brown. They are then very easy to crumble with a rolling pin or in a mortar. They will keep very well in a tightly closed container.

Ready-to-use breadcrumbs can serve the purpose in emergencies, but it is better to make them yourself. Rusks give a slightly sweeter end-product, but the effect is barely noticeable; it seems as if the pâté gets a fuller aroma. I prefer these to breadcrumbs.

Gelatine

A great help for mousses and puddings. Can also be used for jelly, but personally I prefer leg of pig or calf or fishbones and heads to make an aspic jelly. It is a good idea to add a slice of gelatine to make sure you get a good result. I find that gelatine slices are better than powder. Always soak the gelatine in cold water first, before you add it to the tepid liquid. As you stir it will dissolve. If you have any doubts as to whether it is dissolved enough, pour the liquid through a sieve. The undissolved bits will then be left behind.

Stock and court-bouillon

In the old days stock was often used in the forcemeat, nowadays this is rarely done. It is used in fish pâtés, though, and galantines and puddings are cooked in stock. And, of course, stock is the basic ingredient for a jelly. For recipes see *Recipes for pastry, stock and jelly.*

Cream and sour cream

Cream and sour cream are both frequently used in fish pâtés, mousses, or puddings, and in liver and chicken-liver pâté. Cream gives a pâté a softer and fuller flavour. Sour cream (the artificially soured, not the one that you have left to go sour, which is completely different) is less fatty: 20% milk fats, as opposed to whipping cream which contains 40% milk fats. Sour cream has a slightly stronger flavour, which becomes even more pronounced if you add a little lemon juice.

Lemon or orange juice

Both juices add some freshness to a pâté. Orange juice is mainly used in game and poultry pâtés, lemon juice for fish and, sometimes, combined with cream and nutmeg, for meat and liver pâtés.

Alcoholic drinks

In pâté-making it is not the alcohol in a drink that counts, but its aromatic ingredients. Experiment with the various drinks you have in the house. Do not be too economical with your drink, nor too liberal either, for it can ruin the flavour of your pâté. Cognac, armagnac and dry wines are the most popular at present in French cuisine. Port, certain sherries and madeira and occasionally liqueurs, give a slightly sweeter flavour, which can be delicious. Whisky, gin, Dutch gin, calvados, vermouth (preferably a dry one) and cider give a very distinctive aroma, of which you have to be really fond to use it in a pâté. Eau de vie and marc could, if necessary, replace the cognac or armagnac, but the result is not the same. If you haven't any wine or other alcoholic drink in the house, then use a dash of good vinegar to improve the flavour. Wine vinegar and cider vinegar are better than ordinary malt vinegar.

Truffles

Truffles are fungi that grow underground, and which are traced by trained pigs and dogs. They have a penetrating smell and a delicate flavour; they are at their best when fresh, and cannot be kept for very long. The French prefer the black truffles from the Périgord, the Italians prefer the white, Piedmont sort, but these are not so suitable for the long cooking time of pâté. They grow in Southern Europe under oaks and it is almost impossible to cultivate them artificially. That is why they are so rare and, as a result, very expensive. Truffles are sold here and there in tiny tins in delicatessens, but they have little flavour. Should you still wish to give your pâté a typically French 'cachet', then use a tin of truffle cuttings, they are comparatively cheap.

Truffles have the reputation of working as an aphrodisiac, but apart from the psychological effect, which is of course very important,

no one has ever been able to prove this. The truffle was used at Roman feasts.

Nuts, olives, mushrooms, peppers and the like

Almost all kinds of nuts are good in a pâté; walnuts, almonds, hazelnuts, pinenuts and pistachio nuts have all been used in pâtés. Do not use them salted or roasted and blanch them first. This means putting them briefly in boiling water so that the brown skin comes off more easily. Peanuts are not so suitable. Subtropical fruits such as raisins, chopped figs and dates were used particularly in the Middle Ages in pâtés; people were very fond of the combination of sweet and salty, or sweet and sour. (And, to tell you the truth, I rather like it myself.) Olives, filled or unfilled, look very nice and add colour to your pâté, as do strips of red or green pepper, mushrooms and the like.

Herbs, Spices and Salt

Slowly, but surely, most people have now become convinced that herbs and spices are indispensable in the art of cooking. There are many books about herbs on the market and most cookery books now give a list of the most common ones. That is why you will not find a separate list of herbs and spices in this book, only general advice and some classic recipes from French cuisine, which can be used in pâté-making.

Home-ground spices and fresh herbs give the best results. It is better to buy whole seeds and spices, rather than powder, and to grind them yourself in a spare pepper mill, an old coffee grinder or something like that. You can grow fresh herbs in pots, flower boxes or in the garden. In winter they keep excellently in a freezer, which is much better than drying them yourself, as they lose a lot of their aroma that way. If you do not have a freezer, then buy commercial dried herbs. These will have retained more of their bouquet and flavour because of the quicker and better drying methods. Herbs and spices are best bought a little at a time, because no matter how well they are kept, in the long run the quality always deteriorates.

Les quatre épices (the four herbs)

This herb mixture is mentioned in almost all classical French cookery books, without explanation—it is considered to be so well-known. In France it can be easily bought everywhere, and every chef has his own version of the standard recipe. This gives his dishes their own character. The mixture is usually established by experience and experiment or passed on from master to apprentice, when everyone adds or omits something in turn. The official recipe is 7 parts of pepper to 1 part of nutmeg (ground), 1 part of cloves and 1 part of cinnamon; all finely ground and well-mixed. Sometimes 3 parts of allspice are used for the 7 parts of pepper. As far as the flavour is concerned, allspice is a bit like all three spices: nutmeg, clove and cinnamon.

Sometimes cinnamon is substituted for ginger root, also ground. *Larousse Gastronomique* gives the following proportions:

125 gm (5 oz) of white pepper, 10 gm (2 tsp) of cloves, 30 gm (1¼ oz) of ginger and 35 gm (1½ oz) of nutmeg. The name quatre épices is also used for other herb mixtures, but not for those used in pâté making, where the above combination is the usual one. Other mixtures can be thyme, sage, marjoram and basil; or thyme, sage, marjoram and rosemary; or thyme, sage, fennel and rosemary; or any combination of four herbs.

Epices composées (mixed herbs)

Carème gives the following guide for this mixture: take thyme, bay, basil, sage, a little

coriander and mace. Pound all these ingredients, well-dried, in a mortar until fine, and sieve. Add a third of the weight of this mixture in pepper, also finely pounded or ground. Mix everything together thoroughly and store in an air-tight jar.

Chef's herbs (cinque épices)

A combination of thyme, sage, marjoram, nutmeg and pepper.

Sel épicé (spiced salt)

This is a mixture of salt with various herbs and spices, which should be finely pounded and then sieved.

80 gm (3 oz) salt
1 bayleaf
½ tsp peppercorns
a pinch each of cloves, grated nutmeg, cinnamon, dried basil and coriander.

Pound and sift everything once again, so that the ingredients are well mixed. Store in a dry place, covered securely.

Salt and pepper

Your pâté stands or falls on salt. A little too much or not enough can be disastrous. Tasting is the only way to determine whether the amount of salt is right (see next chapter). As a rule of thumb, you can use (10 gm) 2 tsp salt for 500 gm (1¼ lb) of meat. But if ham is worked into the pâté you should definitely use less, as ham is rather salty. I usually use a little less salt than the amount given above, because I like it better that way.

You can use one teaspoon of pepper per tablespoon of salt, depending on your taste and the quality of your pepper. There are different kinds of pepper. Black pepper has retained its skin and has a slightly more aromatic flavour than white pepper. White pepper has lost its skin and is a little hotter, although they belong to the same family, but white pepper is the ripe, and black pepper the unripe fruit. Cayenne pepper is hotter than either and has a different flavour. Cayenne pepper can be combined with one of the other peppers, or used separately. Always grind the pepper the moment you need it, as the aroma is quickly lost. Green pepper should not be ground, but can be used whole or bruised.

General Advice

The most important thing in pâté-making is the end-product which you serve at the table. How you make it is immaterial, but a pâté should be smooth, must have a nice aroma and a delicious flavour and should look attractive. Seeing, smelling and tasting such a dish should make your mouth water.

In order to attain this result every practised pâté-maker has developed his or her own tricks and dodges. Often these are kept religiously secret, but sometimes the makers themselves cannot remember exactly what they have done. So you will have to develop your own expertise. This is essential anyway, because no two ovens are the same; everyone has a different 'touch'; pots, pans and the quality of the ingredients can vary considerably. One butcher's mince is decidedly different from that of his competitor. And mince from the same butcher can differ from day to day, depending on the animals and the scraps he has used at the time.

So, you will have to learn how you can best handle the equipment and raw materials available to you. When I prepare something in my mother's kitchen, for which I even bring my own ingredients, the result is still a little different from when I prepare it at home. I used to shout: 'Mother, you didn't tell me everything', or: 'You are using different ingredients' (this usually was the case, fresher eggs or different-sized ones, another kind of flour or a different brand of drink), but this turned out not to be the only reason. My mother has a different touch and different pans. Her oven operates differently, although the only apparent difference between hers and mine is the year it was made. Your pâtés will not always be the same, even if you think you have kept exactly to the same preparation method and ingredients. At one time you perhaps took longer because a telephone call interrupted the proceedings. And another time you may have been in a 'fat lot I care' mood, and therefore had a slightly freer hand with herbs, spices and salt or drink.

Mood and weather conditions always affect results in cookery: whipping cream, for instance, sometimes won't stiffen at all, and at other times immediately turns to butter. It is just the same with pâté, which is what makes it so exciting. Preparing pâté means experimenting, and tasting as you go along.

Tasting

A bland pâté is extremely dry, and a pâté which is too spicy is not fit to eat. The only way to prevent this is by repeated tasting. There are three methods for a meat filling:

1. At the end of the 'rest period', described below, take a tablespoonful of the mixture, make it into a roll or ball, toss it in some breadcrumbs and fry in a frying pan for 5 minutes, with some butter or fat. Leave till completely cool and taste.
2 At the end of the 'rest period' take a tablespoonful of the filling, wrap it up well in aluminium foil and leave to simmer in boiling water for about 5 minutes, until done. Do not taste until thoroughly cooled. Cooling can be speeded up by putting the bundle in cold water.
3 If you are not averse to tasting raw filling and if you are not afraid of getting worms, then taste a little after the 'rest period'. This method is not as accurate as the two previous ones, because the flavour still changes during the cooking process.

It is better to start off with too few spices and too little salt than with too much of both, as it is simpler to add a little more than to take some out. The only solution in the latter case is to add more fat, meat and/or liver to the filling or, in a hopeless case, breadcrumbs.

In fish, cheese and vegetable pâtés tasting does not present any problems.

The filling

The flavour of the filling is not only determined by the ingredients you use, but also by their texture. The finer the texture, the more the various flavours will blend together. You will notice this if for instance you chop up half of the forcemeat coarsely and the other half very finely, and work them layer by layer into the pâté. A pâté texture can be varied in many ways: by cutting the meat, liver and bacon into the size of cubes you prefer; by chopping up the forcemeat or putting the ingredients through a mincer, in which case you can usually choose between three different kinds of coarseness. Another possibility is to blend the raw materials, already cut into fairly small pieces, into a paste, with an electric blender. The finer the paste is, the better it should be mixed. Do this with a wooden spoon or knead the filling with your hands. Some pâté-makers knead for as long as ten minutes to obtain a homogeneous filling. Strips or cubes of meat, game, liver, kidneys or sweetbread (whether marinated or not) can be stirred through the filling or placed in layers between the filling.

The French call this a *salpicon*. You can do the same with nuts, mushrooms, olives, vegetables and the like. Shrimps, mussels, mushrooms or whatever can be used with fish pâtés in the same way.

'Rest period' before baking

As with ordinary mince a pâté's aroma is greatly enhanced if you let the filling rest in your fridge for at least two hours, but preferably longer. This gives the flavours a chance to blend together because, except when you have aimed for this deliberately, no flavour should be predominant.

Filling the pie dishes

For 1 kilo (2 lb) of meat with flavourings you need a bowl with a capacity of at least 1 litre (2 pints). Do not grease the pie dishes, but line them with pork fat or fresh fatty bacon. This makes for a better aroma and slightly reduces the chance of fat running out of the filling. Also, the pâté will keep better. For a 1 litre (2 pint) pie dish you need 150-200 gm (6–8 oz) of bacon. Should you or your butcher not have cut up the bacon thinly enough, then beat it out a bit more with a wooden hammer.

After putting the filling in the bowl it should be pressed down firmly before you cover the pâté with a few strips of bacon or before you enclose the pâté in the pig's membranes and wrap it up well. Then you can put the lid on or, if you do not have one, a strong piece of kitchen foil. The lid should have a little hole

so that any steam can escape. Professional pâté-makers glue the rim of the lid onto the base with a mixture of rye flour (or ordinary flour) and water.

Lining and filling baking tins

Baking tins should be greased before they are lined with pastry. Most kinds of pastry can be rolled out and then moulded in the tin. Keep a quarter apart for the lid, if this is necessary, or about a third for shallow sandwich tins. Very crumbly pastry can be pressed against the sides, just like hot water crust pastry. Let the pastry stand proud above the edges for one or more centimetres (½ inch). Put the filling in the lined tin and press firmly. The pastry may be first lined with a few strips of fresh fatty bacon, to prevent too much moisture getting into it. (In that case cover the top, too, with a few strips of bacon.)

Fold the edges of the pastry inwards and moisten with milk, water or egg white. Put the pastry lid on top and press the edges firmly. With a fork press small stripes into the edge, this not only looks nice but also makes the edges stick together better. Another method is to let the edges overlap the dish, then put the lid on top and seal the edges together with tweezers. (You can also do it with your fingers.)

From a piece of cardboard or foil, make one or two chimneys, cut circles out of the pastry lid and insert the chimneys. Or prick holes into the lid with a fork, to allow steam to escape. With bits of left-over pastry you can model figures to stick onto the lid with a little egg white, for decoration. Coat the top with a little beaten egg (optional).

You can leave the pâté in the fridge like this for a number of hours; this will only do it good.

Baking

Terrines and pâtés without a crust are in fact not baked; they are cooked *au-bain-marie*. This means that the bowl is placed in a larger bowl or roasting tin, filled with boiling water and put in the oven or on an asbestos mat. This way the temperature in the pâté bowl will remain steadily under 100°C (212°F). A temperature of between 80°–100°C (176°–212°F) is sufficient to let the protein of meat, fish and eggs set.

Pre-heat the oven to 150°C (325°F) and pour boiling water into the roasting tin or a large ovenproof dish. Place the pâté bowl in the water and carefully put everything in the centre of the oven. It is best if the water comes up to a few centimetres (1–2 inches) below the edge of the pâté bowl. The cooking-time will vary from 1 to 2, or sometimes 3 hours, depending on the depth and width of the pâté bowl. Pâtés are done when they withdraw from the sides of the bowl. Another way to test if they are done is to stick a knitting needle into the middle of the filling; if it comes out clean the pâté is done. A pâté should still be quite pink inside,

then it is at its best. Pâté which has been cooked too long is dry and crumbly inside.

Pâtés in pastry are baked. Preheat the oven to 200–225°C (400–440°F) and place the baking tin in the centre of the oven. After 10-15 minutes reduce the heat to 175–200°C (360–400°F) and bake for about 1½ hours. If the top of the crust gets too brown, you can cover it with a piece of foil.

Cooling and storing

Pâtés and terrines are easier to cut if you place a weight on the filling before the fat starts setting during the cooling period. This does not have to be something very heavy; a few tins on a small wooden board are sufficient (and if it causes too many problems you can leave this out altogether). Pâtés and terrines which you want to keep longer than a week should, after cooling, be covered with a layer of melted fat or clarified butter. Cover the bowl securely and place it in the fridge.

Pâtés and terrines are at their best after 1 or 2 days and it is really worth being patient. If you want an elegant layer of jelly around your pâté or terrine, then very carefully scrape the fat (not the set meat juices) from the pâté after it has cooled. Fill up the space left in the bowl with almost, but not quite, set jelly and place the bowl, well-covered, in the fridge. Such a pâté or terrine cannot be kept long, because jelly quickly turns sour. Three days in the fridge is the maximum. If you do not want to eat the pâté for about 5 days, then pour the jelly over the pâté the day before eating.

The hollow space which exists in a cold pâté *en croûte* or a pie is also usually filled with jelly. Pour the cold, but still fluid, jelly through the pie chimney with a funnel after the pâté has cooled, and place it in the fridge, well covered. This must definitely not be kept for more than 3 days.

Never freeze a pâté, terrine, pie or flan. The jelly which formed during baking will break down in the freezer and after defrosting a sodden, watery substance will be all that is left.

Decorating and serving

Decorating a pâté is not really necessary, but it does give the pâté a festive look. If you want a brown crust on your pâté or terrine, then put only very little bacon on top and take the lid or foil off the bowl during the last quarter of an hour of baking. Or place the bowl, without the lid, briefly under the grill.

When the pâté is completely cooled, you can decorate it with a few bay leaves, juniper berries, slices of olive, gherkin or mushrooms or with halved nuts, tangerine or orange segments, slices of hardboiled egg, or cucumber, strips of green or red pepper, or whatever you like. I even saw rose petals on a pâté once, but I don't think those go well with it. Before you put these things on the pâté, first pour a very thin layer of jelly onto it, so that you can 'stick' your decorations on, and let this layer gel before you pour over the rest of the jelly, otherwise the decoration will start shifting about. Let the jelly set well. Serve the decorated pâté very simply, on a bed of lettuce. Always serve your pâté at room temperature. Straight from the fridge a pâté has less flavour.

Recipes for Pastry, Stock and Jelly

'In the absence of bread one eats the pastry crusts' as an old Dutch saying goes. Whether the nice, edible crust is meant, or the hard inedible one in which many pâtés used to be baked, is not clear.

The recipes I give below are for the nice, edible kind. Use ordinary white flour or sieved wholemeal flour, whichever you prefer. Use unsalted butter or margarine and make sure the margarine is hard at fridge temperature. The spreadable-straight-from-the-fridge soft margarine is unsuitable for nearly all kinds of pastry. In most meat pastries you cannot taste the margarine, because rather a lot of fat and meat juices are absorbed by the crust and these will cover up the margarine flavour.

You must realise, when choosing your pastry, that the spicier the flavour of the forcemeat, the less you will be able to taste the flavour of the pastry. For a very delicate pâté or a fish pâté an extra nice pastry crust is more appropriate than for a spicy mince meat pie or a farmhouse pie. Apart from the recipes given here there are, of course, many more kinds of pastry that are suitable for a pâté. And you can make it easy for yourself by using frozen flaky pastry or another kind of ready-to-use pastry—often these products are excellent. The most simple way of making a pâté in a crust is to scoop out a loaf of bread and fill it with forcemeat of your choice.

For a pie which only has a pastry lid you only need half the given amount of pastry. One tablespoon or teaspoon of dry matter always means a level tablespoon or teaspoon. One cupfull is equivalent to 2dl (⅓ pint).

Pastry dough (pâte à pâté) 2 recipes

1
250 gm (10 oz) flour
80 gm (3 oz) lard or 2 tblsp olive oil
3 tsp salt
1 egg yolk
½ cup cold water

2
275 gm (11 oz) flour
80 gm (3 oz) soft butter or margarine
40 gm (1½ oz) lard or fat
2 tsp salt
3 tblsp cold water

Mix the ingredients together with a wooden spoon or with a fork. With cool hands quickly knead the mixture into a ball and place it on a smooth surface. Flatten it with the palm of your hand, while pushing it forward, a kind of rolling movement. Repeat this twice. In this way the dough will be mixed well and will be strong enough to support a heavy filling. Cover the dough, which should be rather firm, and let it rest in a cool place for a few hours, before you roll it out.

Shortcrust pastry (pâte à foncer) 2 recipes

1
250 gm (10 oz) flour
125 gm (5 oz) hard butter or margarine
1 tblsp caster sugar
2 tsp salt
4–8 tblsp ice-cold water
1 beaten egg

2
250 gm (10 oz) flour
100 gm (4 oz) hard butter or margarine
1 tblsp oil
1½ tsp salt
4–8 tblsp ice-cold water
2 beaten eggs

Mix the ingredients together with a fork and very briefly knead them into a ball with your fingertips. This dough can be rolled out or pressed into the tin immediately, but you can also leave it, covered, in the fridge for some time.

Variation leave out the beaten egg in the first version of this recipe. Or leave out the egg and instead of the butter use 75 gm (3 oz) of lard. You can reduce the fat in this recipe to ¼ of the weight of the flour, if you wish. Mix a little grated lemon rind or a tablespoonful of vinegar through the dough.

Wholemeal pastry 2 recipes

1
250 gm (10 oz) wholemeal flour or half wholemeal and half brown rice-flour
6 tblsp butter or margarine
2 tblsp sesame oil
1 tsp salt
2 tblsp water

2
125 gm (5 oz) wholemeal flour
125 gm (5 oz) oat flakes
9 tblsp oil
1 tblsp apple juice
½ tsp salt
a little sesame seed

Mix the dry ingredients together in a mixing-bowl and then add the fat and juice or water. Knead quickly. The dough can be rolled out immediately. Add a tablespoon of honey and/or a little grated lemon rind (optional).

Hot water crust pastry (English recipe for raised pastries and pies) 2 recipes

1
500 gm (1 lb 2 oz) flour
225 gm (9 oz) lard
⅓–½ cup water
2 heaped tsp salt
1½ tblsp caster sugar

2
450 gm (1 lb) flour
100 gm (4 oz) lard
½–⅔ cup water
2 scant tsp salt

Stir the flour and salt together in a mixing bowl and, if you like, the caster sugar. Put the water and the lard in a small saucepan, bring to the boil and, while stirring with a wooden spoon, slowly pour into the flour. It works even better with an electric mixer. Then knead the warm pastry with your hands till it is smooth and supple. If it becomes too warm, cover with a damp teacloth and leave to cool for a while.

If pastry cools too much, it becomes stiff, so feel it every now and again. Put the pastry straight in the tin, while it is still pliable, or as with a raised pie, fold it round inside a tin which has been dusted with flour. Press firmly into all the nooks and crannies so that it takes on the shape of the tin. Cool thoroughly before carefully taking the pastry out of the tin.

Sour cream pastry

350 gm (14 oz) flour
1 egg
150 gm (6 oz) hard butter or margarine
8 tblsp sour cream
1 tsp salt

Mix the flour and the salt in a bowl and work in the hard butter with two knives or a fork. Lightly beat the egg with the sour cream in a separate small bowl, and pour this mixture onto the pastry. Stir thoroughly with a fork until it will form a ball. Cover and let it rest in the fridge for at least an hour, before you roll it out.

Flaky pastry (pâte feuilleté)

200 gm (8 oz) flour
3 tblsp cold water
70–200 gm (3–8 oz) hard butter or margarine
a little salt

The amount of fat needed for flaky pastry can vary from an equal weight of the flour to a third of the weight of the flour. Between these two extremes you can determine the amount of butter yourself. Without kneading too much, make a pastry from the flour, salt and water. Let this rest in the fridge for 15 minutes. It is best if all ingredients and utensils (preferably including the board on which you are going to roll out the pastry) are ice cold. You can put them in the fridge together with the dough. Dust the board and the rolling pin with flour and roll the pastry into a square layer of approximately ½ cm (¼ in) thickness. Put the butter, cut into pieces or slices of ½ cm (¼ in) thickness, on top, and fold the sides inwards. Roll out once again to about the same thickness and fold the layer again. Then back to the fridge for 15 minutes. Repeat this 6 times. The flaky pastry is then ready for use, but you can leave it longer if you like.

Rough Puff pastry (pâte demi-feuilleté)

Use the same ingredients as for the previous recipe, plus the juice of half a lemon. Mix the ingredients together and quickly knead into a ball. The pieces of butter should still be visible. Roll out on a board which has been dusted with flour and fold the layer inwards. Repeat this and place the folded layer in the fridge for 15 minutes or in the freezer compartment for 10 minutes. Repeat this process a few times. (Two to five times is sufficient.)

Curd puff pastry

Add to the ingredients of the previous recipe (rough puff pastry) an equal amount of curd and butter, and set to work in the same way.

Choux pastry 2 recipes

This pastry is delicious filled with a meat, fish or cheese mousse.

1
125 gm (5 oz) flour
100 gm (4 oz) butter or margarine
4 eggs
½ cup water
1 tblsp caster sugar
1 tsp salt

2
125 gm (5 oz) flour
65 gm (2½ oz) butter or margarine
4–5 eggs
½ cup boiled, cooled milk
some fresh ground pepper
1 tsp salt
extra: some grated nutmeg and/or cheese

Put the water, butter, salt and sugar (or milk, butter, salt and pepper) in a large saucepan and bring to the boil. As soon as the liquid boils remove from the gas and add all the sifted flour at once. Keep stirring on a very low gas until you get a smooth substance which comes off the sides. Remove from the gas and stir in the eggs, one by one. Grease a cake tin or other baking mould and spread the pastry in it. Place the tin in a pre-heated oven at 225°C (440°F) and bake for 30—45 minutes. The oven door must definitely not be opened during the first 20 minutes.

   Leave to cool, slice off a lid and scoop it

out. Fill with a mousse. You can also make small choux pastries.

Stock for jelly from meat, game or poultry

Take a calf's knuckle bone or pig's trotters and add the carcass of a bird or scraps of game, (such as the head), small bones from a pork cutlet, a calf's knee or something like that, plus a piece of shin with bone.

Put these in a large pan, together with a few onions, leeks, a winter carrot, or a few small carrots, one or more cloves of garlic, celery, parsley, a bayleaf, a few peppercorns and (optional) some thyme or juniper berries or lemon rind or a few cloves or a combination of these, depending on what you fancy. Add enough water to cover the ingredients; to make something special, you can add a little dry white wine. Absolutely no salt should be added. Very slowly bring the stock to the boil, skim and put the lid on. Now let the stock simmer very, very slowly for about 4 hours. The liquid must not boil, but should be kept just off the boil. Pour the liquid through a sieve. Now the stock can serve as a base for a sauce or jelly (boiled down a little if you like) or, with a little salt, can be served as soup.

Fish stock

Ask your fishmonger for fish heads and bones, skins, fins and the like; 500 gm for 1 litre (1 lb for 2 pints) of liquid is enough. At home, put them in a panful of water and add some celery, parsley, carrots, shallots, leeks, garlic, lemon rind, a bay leaf, a few peppercorns, and (optional) a clove and a little white wine or vinegar. Slowly bring the fish stock to just off the boil and leave to draw like this for 20 minutes. Skim off and pour through a sieve. You can poach fish intended for a mousse or pie in this stock, before you let it cool into a jelly.

Vegetable stock

Take a few potatoes, carrots, onions, leeks, garlic, celery, parsley, and (optional) some cabbage or other vegetables you have in house. Add a few peppercorns, some bay and any other herbs you fancy, and water. Slowly bring the ingredients to the boil, put the lid on the pan and leave to draw for about 1½ hours on a low heat. The stock should be sieved if you are going to use it for jelly, but you always need gelatine for this; it does not automatically gel.

Jelly

Taste the stock you are going to use. There is no salt in it yet, but you can still decide whether the stock has enough flavour. Should this not be the case, then boil the stock down a bit longer on a high heat, without the lid (do not do this with fish stock). This will make the jelly firmer. Next remove every trace of fat.

This is easier if you place the cold stock in the freezer compartment or in the fridge for a little while. You can then also see if the stock gels enough, and if it doesn't you can boil it down a bit more after you have clarified it.

For clarifying take 1 or 2 egg whites, depending on the amount of stock, and beat them until they start to go frothy. Then put the egg whites, together with the stock, in a pan, slowly bring the mixture to just below boiling point (the liquid should be allowed to move just a little bit) and keep it at this temperature for 7–10 minutes. Turn the gas off and leave the stock for another 10 minutes. Next pour the liquid through a warm, damp cloth. The stock should be completely clear. You can now add all sorts of things to the liquid, to taste. In any case, salt should be added, with perhaps port, madeira or a similar drink and finely chopped parsley or tarragon. Let the jelly cool and process further. Should your jelly still turn out soft, because of very warm summer weather, for instance, then add a slice of gelatine, which you have first soaked in cold water and squeezed out.

Jelly with gelatine

Stock that has been extracted without bones (vegetable stock, for instance) needs gelatine to stiffen it. If necessary, clear the stock as given in the previous recipe and add a few slices of gelatine to the warm liquid, after you have soaked them in cold water and squeezed them out. Six gelatine slices for ½ litre (1 pint) of liquid is ample. Flavour the jelly with salt and (optional) other aromatics and leave till thoroughly cool. Jelly cannot be frozen.

If you have made far too much stock, boil it down a bit further and use this *glacé* as a base for sauces. Or freeze it.

Meat Recipes

Some connoisseurs claim that the nicest pâtés come from the Ardennes, the Elzas and the Gascogne. I do not agree with this (although true to tradition, they do make delicious pâtés there) since I have tasted the most exquisite terrines and pâtés in many places throughout Belgium and France. And in various restaurants in Holland, too, I have eaten pâtés and *terrines du chef* which, when I think back, make my mouth water.

The recipes that I describe here are not only from French, Belgian and Dutch cuisines, they come from all over the place. In addition, I have included a number of old recipes, some of them in their original form, not purely out of curiosity or for comparison with modern recipes, but mainly because they are very good. It is really worth giving them a try.

For the forcemeat the proportions of meat and fat vary considerably in the recipes, but as a guideline use as much fatty meat as lean meat. You can obtain a similar result if you take for instance 3 parts of lean meat and 1 part of fat (fresh fatty bacon or butter).

Do not be too sparing with salt, spices, herbs and alcoholic drinks, nor too generous either. A lot of drinks can only be used if you heat them to just below boiling and keep them at that temperature, to allow the alcohol to evaporate and preserve the drink's aroma. If you are going to make a pâté for the first time, you probably won't find it easy. Perhaps the result will not be what you expected. Don't lose heart, and remember that you did not learn to cook in one day either. And in the event that the pâté is a failure, then look at the back of this book to see what you can do to save it.

Pâtés and pastries

Pâtés in a crust and pastries may seem more difficult than terrines, but they are not. If you make a simple pastry it does not involve a lot of extra work and with ready-to-use pastry it is done in a moment. A crisp and brittle crust, into which the flavour of the filling has permeated, is delicious and well worth the trouble.

Most pâtés, without crusts, can be baked as a terrine and vice versa. The filling remains the same. If you want to make small pastries, use more dough in proportion and bake for a shorter time. Half the time for a large pie will usually be enough.

Pâté maison (basic recipe)

This is a typical recipe for the pâté which is served to you in restaurants under the name of *pâté maison* or *pâté du chef*. The list of ingredients looks more complicated than it really is; do not be put off by it. From the options, simply choose the ingredients that appeal to you. For the 'how's' and 'why's' of the preparation method see under 'General advice'.

pastry to choice
400 gm (1 lb) fatty pork (pork steaks, a piece of boned pork cutlet or belly pork)
400 gm (1 lb) lean pork, veal or beef
200 gm (8 oz) pig's liver or another kind of liver
1 clove of garlic, pressed or finely chopped and/or 1 finely chopped fried onion
1 beaten egg
2 tblsp flour or breadcrumbs or Dutch rusk
2 tblsp cognac, armagnac, gin, whisky or the like
1 small glass madeira or dry white wine
about 1 tblsp salt or sel épice
herbs and spices to taste, for instance, quatre épices, chef's herbs, épices composées (for the recipe see under 'Herbs, spices and salt')

Mince or chop up the meat, the liver and the pork into the texture you require (put them once, twice or three times through the mincer, chop them up finely or cut them into small cubes). You can also mix small pork cubes through the rest of the minced filling.

Stir meat, fat and liver together well and add egg, flour (dissolved in a little cognac), cognac, white wine, garlic, salt and spices. Mix everything thoroughly, preferably by kneading it a little, and taste. If necessary, improve the flavour and leave, covered, in a cool place for a few hours. Taste again and improve as necessary. Grease a baking-tin, line it with ⅔ of the pastry and put in the filling. Press it down firmly and stick the pastry lid on top. Make a chimney in the lid, decorate with any left-over bits of pastry and finish off with some egg white or an egg white and water mixture.

Pre-heat the oven to 200–225°C (400–440°F) and place the pâté in the centre of the oven. Reduce the heat to 175–200°C (360–400°F) after 15 minutes in a gas oven or 10 minutes in an electric oven. Total baking time: ¾–1½ hours, depending on the size and height of the pâté. To check if the filling is done you can stick a knitting needle or a knife through the chimney into the filling and if it comes out completely clean, the pastry is done. Leave to cool.

If you like, you can pour some liquid jelly through the chimney of the cooled pâté. 1–2 cups of jelly is sufficient.

Pâté Marry

shortcrust pastry
300 gm (12 oz) pork fillet
1 small glass madeira or sherry
300 gm (12 oz) lean pork
200 gm (8 oz) lean veal
200 gm (8 oz) smoked bacon
200 gm (8 oz) pig's liver
3 eggs
2 tblsp armagnac or cognac
freshly ground black pepper
about 2 tsp salt
2 tsp chopped sage
2 tsp chopped thyme
stuffed olives

Instead of the sage and thyme you can use 2 tsp of tarragon and 2 tblsp of parsley and instead of the armagnac, 2 tblsp of Pernod.

If you are fond of garlic, add 1 or 2 very finely chopped cloves. As you can see, this recipe too offers many possibilities. For instance, stir some tomato purée or ketchup into the mixture, with a little paprika powder and marjoram.

Leave the pastry in the fridge for 24 hours before you use it. Cut the pork fillet into strips or small circles and marinate them for a few hours in the madeira, mixed with some sage and thyme. Mince the rest of the meat, liver and bacon. Stir in the beaten eggs, the marinade and the other ingredients, except the fillet and the olives, and knead well. Taste. Leave a little longer if you like, taste again and season if necessary. Roll out ⅔ of the pastry and line a greased tin with it. Cover the bottom of the pastry with a layer of filling and put another layer against the sides. Put a layer of marinated fillet on the filling (the pieces should not touch each other), and fill up the spaces with olives. Repeat once again with a layer of filling and a layer of fillet and finish with a layer of filling. Roll out the rest of the pastry, for the lid, and fasten to the base. Make two chimneys in the lid, decorate the pastry and coat the top with a little beaten egg.

Pre-heat the oven to 200–225°C (400–440°F), place the pâté in the centre of the oven and reduce the heat to 175–200°C (360–400°F) after 15 minutes (or 10 minutes in an electric oven). Total baking time 1¼–1½ hours. When the meat juices start running from the pastry, it is done. Cool the pâté and after 20 minutes carefully loosen it at the sides, so you can take it out of the tin more easily when it is cool.

Pâté de Chartres en croûte (meat)

There are different kinds of pâté that bear this name. It is no longer possible to trace an original version; they probably made more than one kind of pâté in Chartres.

flaky pastry
500 gm (1¼ lb) boned pork cutlet
200 gm (8 oz) lean veal
100 gm (4 oz) chicken livers
2 large egg yolks
1 cup cream
1 tablsp quatre épices
about 1 tblsp salt
1–2 cups jelly
1 small liqueur glass cognac
1 small liqueur glass port or madeira
100 gm (4 oz) tongue
100 gm (4 oz) ham
100 gm (4 oz) lean veal
100 gm (4 oz) fresh fatty bacon
2 tblsp cognac
a few bruised juniper berries
some freshly ground black pepper (optional)

Cut the tongue, ham, the veal (the 100 gm (4 oz) and the bacon into strips, sprinkle them with the tablespoons of cognac and the juniper berries and leave for a few hours, turning the meat from time to time. Mince the pork cutlet, the veal and the chicken livers very finely, put them three times through the mincer's finest blade, or put everything in an electric blender. Beat in the egg yolks and then the cream. Add the herbs, cognac and madeira. Mix everything thoroughly, leave to rest and taste as described under 'General advice'. Roll out the pastry and line a greased bread tin with two thirds of it. Put a layer of filling on the bottom, then a layer of marinated meat and continue until both have been used up. Finish with a layer of filling. Cover the pâté with the rest of the flaky pastry and attach it firmly. Make two chimneys and decorate it as beautifully as possible. Pre-heat the oven to 200–225°C (400–440°F) after half an hour and bake for just under an hour.

Half an hour after you have reduced the heat, briefly remove the pâté from the oven and coat the lid with a little beaten egg. Let the pâté cool, and after 20 minutes detach the sides from the tin with a knife. When it is thoroughly cooled, pour the (still fluid) jelly through the chimney. If this does not work, then slice off the top of the pâté and pour the jelly over the filling. Put the lid back on and leave the pâté overnight.

Veal pâté

750 gm (1¾ lb) veal mince
250 gm (10 oz) calf's livers
1 onion, finely chopped
1 egg
½ cup sour cream
2 tblsp finely chopped parsley
2–3 tsp salt
½ tsp freshly ground pepper
a little grated nutmeg
2 tblsp madeira
15 coarsely chopped almonds
flaky pastry

Mince the liver and the meat very finely together. Stir the remaining ingredients into the mince and mix well. Put it aside. Roll out the flaky pastry and line a baking tin with two thirds of this. Coat the inside with some beaten egg white. Spoon the filling into the tin and cover the pâté with the rest of the pastry. Make two chimneys in the lid, decorate it and coat with beaten egg or egg-white. Place the pâté in a 200–225°C (400–440°F) pre-heated oven and after 20 minutes reduce the heat to 175–200°C (360–400°F). Total baking time about 1 hour. If you like, you can pour some jelly with madeira into the crust, after the pâté has cooled.

Meat pâté with cheese

This is a recipe from the cookery book *De honesta voluptate* (About true enjoyment) by Platina, a librarian at the Vatican Library during the time of Pope Sixtus IV (1471 to 1484). The translation of the original recipe is as follows:

'Boil meat, either from a calf or a billy-goat or a nanny-goat, and when it is done and boned, cut it into pieces and pound it in a mortar. Next add a little soft cheese and an equal amount of mature, grated cheese, some chopped parsley and marjoram, 15 well-beaten eggs, belly-pork or calf's udders, a little pepper, a little more cinnamon, very little ginger, as much saffron as necessary to give it colour. Cook this in the same way as for a white tart. Scaurus and Celius, who are so eager to exchange their skinny figures for fat ones, should eat this. It is not very nourishing, makes the body fat, is good for the liver, causes constipation and kidney stones.'

Take 500 gm (1¼ lb) of knuckle of veal, and 250 gm (10 oz) of chopped-up udder, cooked in stock until done, 50 gm (2 oz) of soft cheese and an equal amount of mature cheese, 4–5 eggs and the indicated spices. Thoroughly mix the ingredients together, in a mortar or an electric blender. Taste and season.

In the old days people could not make flour as white and as fine as they can now and therefore wholemeal flour seems to be eminently suitable for this recipe. Use enough pastry for a closed flan, line a greased mould with ⅔ of the pastry and spoon in the filling. Close the pâté, make two chimneys in the lid and decorate it with left-over pieces of pastry.

Bake the pâté in a moderately hot oven 175°C (350°F) for ¾ hour.

Variation Mix a few sliced mushrooms and a fried onion and/or garlic into the filling, or use a sour-cream dough.

You could also mix in a few chopped-up dates, figs and raisins. In that case, a dash of vinegar is very nice in the filling.

Meat-loaf Amsteldijk

Another recipe that offers all kinds of possibilities. It is very simple to make. This meat-loaf has never turned out the same twice when I have made it, because I just put in what I happen to have in the house or what I feel like on the spur of the moment. You may think it is a rather vague recipe, but this time the quantities of herbs can be used rather freely.

Start with a simple mixture, a standard pastry dough, shortcrust pastry or hot-water crust pastry. Use the proportions that are given in the chapter 'Recipes for pastry, stock and jelly'. Then make a fried filling from:

250 gm (10 oz) pork mince
250 gm (10 oz) beef mince
1 clove finely pressed garlic
1 very finely chopped onion
raisins, as many as you like
salt, cayenne pepper and black pepper
1 tblsp brown sugar or ginger juice
some ginger powder
some marjoram and/or oregano
some coriander
some parsley
2 eggs
2 crumbled rusks
a dash of vinegar and/or some tamarind
strips of vegetables for the colour, such as red pepper or tomato or carrot, mushrooms or green pepper

Sometimes I add a dash of soy sauce or a little tomato-purée and some thyme, sage, mace and cloves. Or I use some curry powder.

Fry the onion and the garlic in a little olive oil, in a large saucepan, add the mince and loosen it with a fork. Stir in the raisins, as well as the herbs and spices. Fry for a while and then remove the pan from the heat. Mix the beaten eggs with the vinegar and (optional) the soy sauce or tomato purée. Stir this mixture through the mince when it has cooled a little, then add the rusks and finally the strips of vegetable. Taste carefully and adjust the flavour as necessary.

Roll out the pastry, put the mince mixture in the middle, press it firmly and close up the pastry on all sides. Or line a cake tin with two thirds of the pastry, spoon in the mince mixture, press it in firmly and fasten the pastry lid on top. Make two chimneys in the lid or prick a pattern of holes in it with a fork.

Place the meat loaf in a pre-heated oven at 200–225°C (400–440°F) and bake it for 45–60 minutes. When the crust is yellow-gold, the pâté is done. This meat loaf is just as nice warm or cold.

Mince Pâté with capers

This is the same kind of recipe as the previous one, the difference being that the mince mixture is placed raw into the pastry crust. That makes tasting a little more difficult. Think up your own variations, too.

wholemeal pastry or sour cream pastry
250 gm (10 oz) pork mince
250 gm (10 oz) beef mince

a few chicken-livers (optional)
1 finely chopped onion
1 beaten egg
1 tblsp sour cream
salt
freshly ground black pepper
some ground caraway seed
some finely chopped carrot
2 tblsp flour or breadcrumbs
paprika powder (optional)
capers

Fry the onion and the carrot briefly in some butter and leave to cool. Chop up the chicken-livers very finely and mix the ingredients thoroughly. Now leave the mince for a while and then taste as described under 'General advice'. If necessary, season the mixture and taste again. Roll out the pastry, line a baking tin (a turban mould looks very nice) with two thirds of the pastry and spoon in the mince mixture. Press in firmly and fasten the lid. Place the pâté in a pre-heated oven at 200–225°C (400–440°F) and bake for 45–60 minutes, until done. When the pastry crust is yellow-gold, the pâté is done. If the top colours too much, place a piece of aluminium foil loosely over the pâté. Serve hot or cold.

Persian patties

These small patties are still often made in the Middle East; the recipe is very old. They are described in the book by Al-Baghdadi, from 1226. This man divided enjoyment into six classes: food, drink, clothes, sex, smell and sound. The most important and most noble of all was food, according to him. He placed the enjoyment of food way above any other form of enjoyment and this was his reason for writing the book.

Make a hot-water crust pastry from:
450 gm (1lb 2oz) flour
125 gm (5 oz) butter or margarine
6 tblsp sesame oil
5 tblsp water
some salt

Put the pastry in a cool place while you make the filling.

250 gm (10 oz) cooked minced beef
5 tblsp water
a little lemon juice
salt and freshly ground pepper
2 tblsp coriander
½ tsp cummin
mint, dried or fresh
50 gm (2 oz) chopped walnuts or pinenuts
1 small egg

Put the mince, water, lemon juice, salt, pepper, coriander, cummin and mint together in a pan, bring to the boil and simmer for 15 minutes. The mixture should be damp, not wet. Add the walnuts. Take the pan from the heat, let the mixture cool a little and stir in the beaten egg.

Roll out the pastry, cut it into squares and make envelopes or ordinary triangles. Or shape it in such a way that you get small pastry cups with lids. Put a little filling between the pastry or in the cups. Wet the sides with egg white, milk or water and press them together firmly. Coat the patties with a little beaten egg. Put them on a greased baking sheet and place it in a pre-heated oven at 175–200°C (350–400°F). Bake them for about ½ hour.

Or fry the triangles in hot oil till they are golden brown on both sides.

Empanades (Spanish patties)

These patties have all kinds of fillings. Sometimes one large 'pie' is made. I have only mentioned the unusual fillings here. Take pastry of your choice, roll it out and make envelopes, triangles or small cups with lids.

Put in one or two of the fillings described below and bake them as described for the previous recipe.

Pumpkin-beef filling

200 gm (8 oz) cooked mince beef
1 tblsp brown sugar
200 gm (8 oz) pumpkin
½ tsp clove powder
50 gm (2 oz) pine-nuts or almonds, blanched and chopped
½ tsp cinnamon
50 gm (2 oz) raisins
some salt
freshly ground pepper

Peel the pumpkin and cut it into small cubes. Boil the cubes in a little water with salt until done, drain them and make a purée. Mix the purée with the other ingredients.

Apricot-pork filling

150 gm (6 oz) minced pork
50 gm (2 oz) chopped, roasted almonds
100 gm (4 oz) cooked and chopped apricots
some salt
½ tsp sugar
a little stock
100 gm (4 oz) currants and raisins

Mix the ingredients thoroughly.

Lamb filling

200 gm (8 oz) cooked minced lamb
50 gm (2 oz) fresh fatty bacon, minced
50 gm (2 oz) minced Spanish sausage
a little fresh thyme
some grated orange rind
some grated lemon rind
some salt
freshly ground pepper

Mix the ingredients thoroughly, moisten them with a little stock (optional) and let the filling stand for some time.

Cider-tongue filling

200 gm (8 oz) cooked and minced tongue
some salt
50 gm (2 oz) finely pounded almonds
a pinch of nutmeg
50 gm (2 oz) chopped raisins
a pinch of clove powder
some cider

Mix the ingredients thoroughly and let the mixture rest for some time.

Moroccan pie

See shortcrust pastry or wholemeal pastry. For the filling you need:

250 gm (10 oz) finely chopped lamb
250 gm (10 oz) finely chopped beef
olive oil
2 sliced tomatoes
2 sliced aubergines
salt and a pinch of cayenne pepper
some quatre épices
1 tblsp brown sugar
3 tblsp tamarind or lemon juice
3 tblsp parsley
raisins (optional)
an egg with some breadcrumbs (optional)

Fry the meat in the olive oil until brown and add salt, pepper, tomato and aubergines. Fry this mixture for a while and then add the rest of the ingredients, except the egg with breadcrumbs. Remove the pan from the heat and, if you like, add the beaten egg with breadcrumbs. Line a greased ovenproof dish with two thirds of the pastry and spoon in the mixture. Fasten the rest of the pastry onto the pie and make two chimneys in the lid. Bake in a moderately warm oven for about an hour.

Variation use brains instead of aubergines. The brains should first be soaked in water with 1 spoonful of vinegar, for an hour. Rinse them under running water and remove the membrane. Bring water with salt and 1 spoonful of vinegar to the boil, add the brains and simmer for about 10 minutes. Then drain and mash with a fork. Do not stir the brains into the meat mixture until they have cooled a little. The egg can also be mixed in hard-boiled.

Mousse de foie en croûte

A light pâté which is made in a baked crust of choux pastry. (For the latter, see under 'Recipes for pastry, stock and jelly.)

250 gm (10 oz) calf's livers
50 gm (2 oz) fresh fatty bacon
½ finely chopped onion
3 eggs, separated into yolk and white

½ cup cream
1 tblsp cognac or similar
½ pressed clove of garlic
a little salt
a little freshly ground pepper
some parsley
some thyme (optional)
100 gm (4 oz) mushrooms

Cut the liver and the bacon into cubes and briefly fry them. Scoop the mixture from the pan and fry the onion, garlic and mushrooms in the remaining fat. Add the cognac, simmer for a little while and remove the pan from the heat. Pound the liver and bacon as finely as possible in a mortar, through a drum sieve or an electric blender. Now add the remaining ingredients, except the egg whites. Stir thoroughly, taste and season. Beat the egg whites till stiff and spoon them through the mixture. Pour or spoon the mixture into the pastry crust, loosely put the lid on top and bake the pâté in a pre-heated oven at 175–200°C (350–400°F) for about an hour. You can see if the pâté is done by sticking a knife into the filling; if it comes out clean the pâté is ready.

Variation use some chopped-up hazelnuts instead of mushrooms, or use fresh green peppercorns.

Calf's sweetbread pâté

The refined flavour of this pâté is done most justice if you serve it hot. Dish it up with a shrimp sauce or a lobster sauce: these are classic combinations.

Use shortcrust pastry. For the filling you need

400 gm (1 lb) calf's sweetbread
300 gm (12 oz) lean pork
300 gm (12 oz) fresh fatty bacon
2 large eggs
1 heaped tbsp flour
½ cup cream
freshly ground pepper and thyme
a little Worcester sauce or white wine to taste
100 gm (4 oz) edible fungi (mushrooms, boletus, dried cep or something like that)
50 gm (2 oz) butter
about 1 tsp salt

Soak the sweetbreads in cold water with salt for an hour. Then cook them in some chicken stock with a little lemon juice (added to the cold stock) until done (about 20 minutes). Drain them and remove the skins and dark patches. Cut them into small pieces.

You can make the mince filling while the sweetbreads are cooking. Mince the meat and the fat as finely as possible. An electric blender is best for this. Add the beaten eggs, flour, and cream and stir well. Season with salt, pepper, thyme and, if you like, Worcester sauce. Slice the fungi and briefly fry them in butter. If you have a lot of them, mix a few into the filling.

Roll out the pastry and line a greased

baking tin with a thin layer of it. Put half of
the mince filling on the bottom, put the
sweetbreads and fungi on top and finish off
with the rest of the filling. Lay a pastry lid on
the pâté, decorate it with bits of left-over
pastry, make two chimneys in the lid and coat
with a little beaten egg.

Bake the pâté in a moderately hot oven at
175°C (350°F) until done (about an hour).

Variation use a tin of oysters, drain them,
halve them and put them between the pieces
of sweetbread. Or put mussels between the
sweetbread. Artichoke hearts are another
possibility. Hazelnuts are also supposed to be
very good. Or use some chef's herbs instead
of thyme.

Terrines

It is best not to make terrines in small pots. The chance that all the meat juices will run from the filling and you will be left with a dry meat ball is much greater than with the proportions that I give. The previous pâté and pie recipes can also be baked as terrines and can therefore be kept longer.

Terrine maison

400 gm (1 lb) calf's, pork or beef (minced)
400 gm (1 lb) belly pork
1 finely chopped and fried onion
½ cup dry white wine
some thyme
some marjoram
some ground cloves
some grated nutmeg
a pinch of cayenne pepper
salt and freshly ground pepper
100 gm (4 oz) cooked tongue
rashers of fresh fatty bacon

You can alter the proportions of meat, liver and fat a little. For instance, use leaner pork and 150 gm (6 oz) of fresh fatty bacon. Grind up the meat and the liver finely—two or three times through the mincer. Add the other ingredients except the ox tongue and the bacon rashers. Mix everything well and leave in a cool place for a few hours. Taste as described under 'General advice' and, if necessary, improve the flavour. Taste again.

Cut the ox tongue and (optional) a little bacon into cubes and stir through the filling. Line the pie dish with strips of bacon and spoon in the filling. Press down a little and cover the terrine with some bacon. If you like, you can put a few bayleaves and juniper berries on top of the filling. Put the lid on the dish and seal with a little rye dough. Or cover the dish with aluminium foil, preferably two layers.

Now bake the terrine *au-bain-marie* in a moderately hot oven at about 175°C (350°F) until done (about 1½ hours). Let it cool and after a while put a weight on top. The terrine should be left for at least 24 hours and preferably 48 hours.

Variation use some sel épicé instead of the salt and spices. Add 1 or 2 eggs, a little cream and some flour to the filling. Also a clove of garlic and a dash of some strong drink. Add a little sage. Or, instead of the ox tongue, use some chopped up kidneys and heart.

Country terrine

400 gm (1 lb) cooked lamb
300 gm (12 oz) sausage meat
3 tblsp bacon cubes
3 slices brown bread without crusts
some milk
2 beaten eggs
1 very finely chopped onion
1 or 2 cloves finely chopped garlic

1 tblsp chopped olives
1 tblsp chopped parsley
1 or 2 tblsp cognac, madeira or port
salt and freshly ground black pepper

Soak the bread in some milk and squeeze it out a little before mixing it into the filling. Put the meat and the sausage meat through the mincer, or chop it up very finely. Mix in the rest of the ingredients. Taste well and, if you like, add some herbs and spices of your choice. Let the filling rest for a while and taste again. Grease a pie dish, and spoon in the filling. Put the lid on the dish and place the terrine in a moderately hot oven at 150–175°C (325–350°F). Bake it for about an hour, the last 30 minutes without the lid.

Ardenne terrine

A smooth, coarse-grained pâté from Bouillon, a beautiful little town with an impressive castle, on the border of Belgium and France, where you can eat delicious food.

250 gm (10 oz) lean pork
250 gm (10 oz) fatty pork
250 gm (10 oz) veal
250 gm (10 oz) chicken-livers
about 2 tsp salt
2 tsp freshly ground pepper
2 tsp cognac, rum or madeira

Chop up the four kinds of meat as finely as possible, with a large sharp kitchen knife. Do not mince the meat, as this would spoil the flavour and the texture. Add the other ingredients, mix thoroughly, and spoon into a greased ovenproof dish or pie-dish. Cover the terrine and let it rest in the fridge for a while. Taste and adjust the flavour if necessary.

Press the filling down a little and put a few sprigs of fresh thyme, a bay-leaf and fresh fatty bacon, cut like matchsticks, on top. Cover the dish with aluminium foil, two layers.

Place the terrine in a baking tin or roasting tin filled with water, (the water should reach the middle of the dish) and place in a moderately hot oven at 180°C (360°F). Cook the terrine for about an hour, without the foil for the last 20 minutes. Let it cool and place it, well covered, in the fridge for another 2 hours. If necessary, this terrine can be served cold.

Coarse Ardenne terrine

250 gm (10 oz) fatty veal
125 gm (5 oz) fatty pork
125 gm (5 oz) pig's liver
1 finely cut clove of garlic
a little ground bay
a pinch of nutmeg
1 tsp chopped parsley
¼ tsp freshly chopped thyme
salt and freshly ground pepper
1 or 2 tblsp cognac or eau de vie
1 or 2 tblsp white wine
some juniper berries (optional)

Follow the same method as described for the previous terrine, but do not chop up the meat and liver too finely. If you like, add some fresh fatty bacon.

Farmland terrine

250 gm (10 oz) calf's liver
500 gm (1¼ lb) minced veal
1 onion
1–2 cloves garlic
1 full tblsp tomato purée
1 tblsp chopped savory
2 tsp chopped oregano
100 gm (4 oz) soft butter or margarine
¼ cup red wine
salt and freshly ground pepper
1 tblsp parsley
200 gm (8 oz) streaky bacon or fresh fatty bacon, thinly sliced

Chop up the liver and onions, cut the garlic very finely and mix together all the ingredients except the bacon. Taste, leave the mixture for a few hours and taste again.

Line a pie-dish with two thirds of the bacon slices, spoon the filling into the dish, press it down a little and lay some bacon on top. Put the lid on the dish and place it, *au-bain-marie*, in a pre-heated oven at about 180°C (360°F). Cook the terrine for about 1½ hours. Then cool, and after about 20 minutes place a weight on the filling. Do not eat the terrine for 2 or 3 days.

Danish Liver Pâté

This Danish liver pâté is almost a national dish. The Norwegians and Swedes make it slightly differently but stick to the combination of liver and fish. It is usually served with a Scandinavian cold buffet or a smorrebrod.

2 tblsp flour
2 tblsp butter
1½ cups whipping cream
1½ cups milk
500 gm (1¼ lb) fresh pig's liver
350 gm (14 oz) fresh fatty bacon
1 onion
rashers of fresh fatty bacon for lining
3 anchovy fillets, drained, or
3 tsp anchovy paste
2 eggs
1½ tsp salt
¾ tsp freshly ground pepper
½ tsp allspice
¼ tsp ginger or clove powder

Melt the butter in a pan, stir in the flour off the heat and then the cream and milk. Bring back to the boil, continuously stirring or beating, until you have a thick smooth sauce. Let it cool. Cut the liver, bacon, onion and, if you like, the anchovy fillet into small pieces. With a little of the cream sauce make it into a purée in an electric blender. Do not put everything into the blender at once, but start with perhaps a third. Mix everything together again, and stir in the beaten eggs, herbs and the rest of the cream sauce. It should become a smooth mixture, easy to pour.

Line a terrine or bread-tin with the slices of bacon and pour in the filling. Cover the mixture with bacon and put a double layer of aluminium foil on top.

Bake the terrine in a pre-heated oven at about 175°C (350°F) *au-bain-marie* for 1½ hours. Let it cool without the aluminium foil. Then put the foil back on, put it in the fridge and serve cold.

Liver cheese

500 gm (1¼ lb) pig's livers
500 gm (1¼ lb) belly pork or neck
50 gm (2 oz) flour
about ¼ cup stock
omentum
1 tblsp salt
2 tsp pepper
1 tsp clove powder
a few cubes of back bacon (optional)

Mince the meat and the liver very finely, twice or three times. Add the rest of the ingredients except the omentum and mix well. Line a mould with the omentum, spoon in the filling and cover. Bake the liver cheese in a pre-heated oven at about 175°C (350°F) *au-bain-marie* for about 1½ hours.
Cool.

Italian liver cheese (Fromage d'Italie)

500 gm (1¼ lb) pig's livers
500 gm (1¼ lb) belly pork
1 large egg
3 tblsp flour
salt and freshly ground pepper
chopped parsley
chopped thyme
chopped sage
5 tblsp dry white wine
or 3 tblsp dry vermouth
and 2 tblsp cognac
some grated nutmeg
some ground cloves
100 gm (4 oz) pistachio nuts
omentum

See previous recipe for preparation.

Mongolian meat-loaf

This recipe dates from the time of the Yuan dynasty, 1274–1356. It does not have the pretensions of a *haute cuisine*, according to the Chinese. The blended flavours of cheese, meat, onion and sesame oil and seeds is supposed to remind one of the flavours and aromas of the steppes of Central Asia (Unfortunately, I have never been there).

450 gm (1 lb 2 oz) lean lamb
450 gm (1 lb 2 oz) lamb's livers and kidneys
1 large onion
625 gm (1½ lb) potatoes or yam

2 slices of ginger root, chopped
2 eggs
4 tblsp cornflour
2 tsp salt
pepper to taste
3 tblsp butter or fat
2 tblsp soy sauce
2 tblsp vinegar
4 tblsp breadcrumbs
4 tblsp grated goat cheese or
Parmesan or Cheddar
2 tsp brown sugar
2 tblsp sesame seeds
6 tblsp sesame oil

Keep the sesame oil and seeds apart from the
rest. Chop up all the ingredients very finely.
Mix everything well and shape it into a loaf.
Press the sesame seeds on it, covering all
sides. Fry the loaf on all sides in a saucepan,
with the sesame oil, until nicely brown and
then bake it in a pre-heated oven at 200–
225°C (400–440°F) until done (about ½ hour).

Pâté de cervelle

1 set of calf's brains
50 gm (2 oz) shelled pistachio nuts or
almonds
1 medium size onion
4 eggs
some finely chopped chervil
about ½ cup stock or milk
some finely chopped tarragon
salt and freshly ground pepper

Soak the brains in cold water for at least an
hour. Rinse them in running water and blanch
them for 5 minutes in boiling water
with a little salt. Rinse again in cold water,
drain and remove the skins and membranes.
make a purée of the brains or cut them into
pieces. Chop up the onion very finely and fry
it in a little oil, together with the parsley,
chervil and tarragon. Let it cool. Beat the eggs
and mix all the ingredients. Put everything in a
greased pie-dish or baking tin and bake the
terrine in a pre-heated oven at 175°C (350°F)
au-bain-marie for half an hour to three
quarters of an hour. Leave to cool.

Variation Stir some breadcrumbs, which have
been soaked in milk, through the filling, and
the juice of half a pressed clove of garlic.

Pies and Flans

Steak and kidney pie

One of the most popular pies in and outside
England, which has a number of regional
variations. For instance, in the West Country
they pour a cupful of double cream through the
chimney, before serving it. In the Scottish
Highlands the pie is spiced with Worcester
sauce, vinegar and tomato purée. Sometimes
mushrooms are mixed in and red port or
wine.

A *steak and kidney pudding* has the same
filling as the pie, but is completely enclosed in
a different kind of crust, made with suet.

shortcrust pastry, hot water crust pastry
or flaky pastry
500 gm (1¼ lb) lean stewing beef
250 gm (10 oz) calf's or ox kidneys
2 full tblsps flour
salt and pepper
1 tblsp chopped parsley
a little frying fat or margarine
1 large finely chopped onion
1½ cups meat stock or half wine and half stock
salt and pepper

Cut the meat and the kidneys into small
cubes. Mix the flour with a little pepper and
salt, toss the cubes in this mixture, so that all
the sides are dusted, and add the parsley.

Melt the frying fat, fry the onions in it and
the meat, until light brown. Pour over the
stock and simmer gently. 1 to 1½ hours is
enough.

Next put everything in an ovenproof dish,
cover it with a pastry lid, make a chimney in it
and coat the lid with a little beaten egg. Bake
the pie in a pre-heated oven at 200°C (400°F)
until the crust is golden brown.

Sometimes the pie is cooked entirely in the
oven, but then it should bake for about
2½ hours.

Steak, kidney and oyster pie

Add a dozen chopped oysters, with their juice,
to the above pie before putting the pastry lid
on top.

Devon pork pie

shortcrust pastry
6 boned pork chops
3 chopped onions or chopped leeks
6 pippin apples, not too large
and cut into slices
some chopped dried plums
some nutmeg and allspice
2 tblsp sugar
3 cups stock, cider or white wine
salt and freshly ground pepper

You can leave the chops whole (if they are
very thick, cut them across) or cut them into

cubes. Grease an ovenproof dish and put half of the meat on the bottom. Then a layer of apple, sprinkled with a little sugar and/or plums, and on top of that the onions with salt and pepper. Repeat the three layers and add the stock, cider or wine. Make a lid from the dough and fasten it onto the dish. Coat it with a little milk and put the pie in a pre-heated oven at about 200°C (400°F). Reduce the heat after 15 minutes to about 175°C (350°C) and put aluminium foil over the pie. Bake for another 1 to 1¼ hours. Serve covered with warm cream if you like, but this is rather rich.

Variation use lamb instead of pork and a pinch of mace and cinnamon. Then make the pastry with half butter and half lamb's fat and you have a *Devonshire squab pie*. Another possibility is to replace the herbs with sage for the pork and rosemary for the lamb.

Florentine pie

A recipe from *The British Cook's Companion* (1729) by Henry Howard. Take a leg or shoulder of mutton, cut it into pieces and spice with nutmeg, pepper and salt; fry briefly and put it in a dish, together with 3 or 4 shallots, a bag of sweet herbs (thyme, rosemary, chervil, tarragon or whatever you like), 2 or 3 anchovies, 20 small meat balls, 1½ cups of claret (red bordeaux), an equal amount of water; add 225 gm (9 oz) of butter, cover with flaky pastry and bake.

The Scots make it into a *Veal flory* by using veal, no anchovy but bacon, hard-boiled egg yolks or sweetbread and truffles or mushrooms.

Tamale pie (from the American kitchen)

4 cups water
1 green pepper
some salt
4 tomatoes
125 gm (5 oz) cornflour
50 gm (2 oz) butter
50 gm (2 oz) black olives, chopped
450 gm (1 lb 2 oz) minced beef
1 finely chopped onion
1 tsp chilli powder
salt

Bring the water to the boil with a small teaspoon of salt and stir in the cornflour. Put a lid on the pan and simmer very gently for half an hour. Stir occasionally. Mix in the olives and cool. Melt the butter in a pan, fry the onion, add the green pepper, in strips, and then the meat. Stir well. When the meat is brown, add the sliced tomatoes, the chilli powder and seasoning.

Put half of the cornflour on the bottom of an ovenproof dish, put the meat mixture on top and cover with the rest of the cornflour. Put a few thin slivers of butter on top and bake this pie for half an hour in an oven at 175°C (350°).

To make a calf tongue's pie

'Take a calf's tongue/cooked and cleaned/so that there is nothing but tongue/chop it fine with 12 peeled sour apples without cores/add a crumbled Dutch rusk/three quarters part of currants/nutmeg/ginger/and cinnamon/ with a little sugar/then bake it in your crust/and you will find it delicious.'

This is a recipe from *De Verstandige Kock, of Sorghvuldig Huyshoudster*, (The Sensible Cook, or Careful Housekeeper), printed in 1667.

Greek pie

Use a wholemeal dough with some grated lemon rind and a little honey. Plus:
250 gm (10 oz) boned leg of lamb
1 finely chopped onion
fresh mint
1 tblsp brown sugar
juice of ½ lemon
1 egg
1 clove garlic, pressed
salt and freshly ground pepper
400 gm (1 lb) minced lamb
100 gm (4 oz) lamb's liver or chicken livers
juice of ½ lemon
1 clove of garlic
1 slice brown bread
1 tblsp olive oil

Marinate the leg of lamb, cut into cubes, in a mixture of lemon, garlic, olive oil and the chopped up mint. Leave for a few hours. Then quickly fry them in olive oil, until almost done.

Cut the liver very fine and make a firm filling with the rest of the ingredients. Add the marinade of the leg of lamb and taste. Roll the pastry out into pieces. Put one in a greased baking tin and put half the filling on top. Leave a wide edge all round. Put the leg of lamb on the filling and cover with the rest of the mince. Press down a little and coat the edge of the pastry with egg white or milk. Put the second piece of pastry on top and press the edges firmly on to each other. Make a chimney in the lid, or prick a few holes in it with a fork. Coat the pie with a little beaten egg. This pie can also be made in a round pie-dish.

Now leave it for a while. Preferably a few hours.

Pre-heat the oven to 200–225°C (400–440°F), place the pie in the centre of the oven. After 15 minutes reduce the heat to 175–200°C (350–400°F) (after 10 minutes in an electric oven). The total baking time is about three quarters of an hour. Cool the pie a little before taking it out of the baking tin and serving it.

Variation use fresh rosemary instead of mint.

Pork pie with spinach or stinging nettles

Instead of spinach or stinging nettles you can use all kinds of different vegetables that appeal to you. (A layer of mixed vegetables or a layer of beans or cauliflower, for instance.)

500 gm (1¼ lb) minced pork
4 beaten eggs
100 gm (4 oz) grated cheese
Parmesan or Swiss cheese
salt and freshly ground pepper
a pinch of saffron (optional)
some ginger powder
some grated nutmeg
some ground cardamom
1 pressed clove of garlic
750 gm (1¾ lb) cooked fresh spinach or
stinging nettles, with a little sorrel

Mix the ingredients, except the spinach, thoroughly, taste and season. Line a greased pie dish with ⅔ of the pastry. Put half of the mince mixture on top, and on top of that the well-squeezed spinach and sorrel. Spoon the rest of the mince mixture over it and close the pie with the rest of the pastry. Make a chimney in the lid and put a few thin slices of butter on top. Bake the pie in a pre-heated oven at 175–200°C (350–400°F) for about an hour. You can also serve the pie cold, but it is nicer hot.

Variation use different spices or stir some cream through the mince.

Sundries

Mousse de jambon

250 gm (10 oz) boiled ham without fat
1 cup jelly
2 tblsp flour
1½ cups whipping cream
2 tblsp butter
salt and cayenne pepper or
freshly ground pepper
milk
1 glass madeira
2 egg whites

Mince the ham as finely as possible. Melt the butter in a saucepan and add the flour. Pour in the milk, little by little, until you have a thick sauce, and add the madeira. Boil for a little while and then cool.

Mix the ham and the sauce in an electric blender or rub the ham in a mortar until fine. Then add the sauce and the fluid, still luke-warm, jelly. Whip the cream, mix it in and season to taste. Taste carefully. Beat the egg whites till stiff, carefully fold them into the mixture and put the mousse in an attractive dish in the fridge. Serve chilled, and just before serving take the foil from the bowl so the mousse looks like a raised soufflé.

Variation leave out the jelly and cream, remove from heat and stir two egg yolks through the sauce. Put the mousse in small soufflé bowls, sprinkle some cheese over the top and cook the mousses in the oven *au-gratin* for about 10 minutes.

This mousse can also be made from boiled tongue and ham or from boiled chicken and tongue or left-overs of game, poultry or meat.

Veal galantine

Take a nice piece of calf's breast without bone. The meat should not be too thick and should be big enough to be wrapped around the filling. For the filling you need:

250 gm (10 oz) lean minced pork (or pork and veal, or veal and ham)
250 gm (10 oz) fatty minced pork
some pistachio nuts, truffle cuttings, mushrooms, pieces of sweetbread or something like that
fresh herbs, but not too many and not mixed —use either basil and parsley or just parsley, or marjoram, or thyme and parsley
2 eggs
salt and pepper

You also need stock, for the recipe see the chapter 'Recipes for pastry, stock and jelly.'

Mix the ingredients for the filling thoroughly. Fold the meat double and sew it together on two sides. Put the filling between the meat and sew the third side. Push the meat back into shape. You can leave it for a few hours, if you like.

Then tie the meat in a piece of cheesecloth

or a napkin, by rolling it inside and tying the ends firmly.

The stock should have been boiling for at least two hours before you add the meat. Gently simmer it in the stock for about 2 hours. Do not take the galantine from the stock until it is fully cooled. Take off the napkin, make a little jelly with the stock and put a thin layer of this over the galantine. Serve surrounded by some chopped jelly.

Haggis

This national Scottish dish is a pudding of sheep's heart, lungs, and liver, with lard, oatmeal and onions, cooked in a sheep's stomach. The poet Robert Burns even sang of it in his poem *To a Haggis* in 1786. And although the Scots are very proud of it, this Haggis was already made in the time of Homer.

1 sheep's stomach
1 sheep's heart
sheep's lungs (can be left out)
1 sheep's liver
250 gm (10 oz) fresh suet
100 gm (4 oz) oat-meal, lightly roasted
a little lemon juice or vinegar
3 finely chopped onions
1–2 tsp salt
freshly ground pepper
cayenne pepper
grated nutmeg
1½ cups strongly concentrated stock or meat gravy

Clean the organs thoroughly, except the stomach, and put in clean cold water. Bring to the boil, if necessary change the water, and with the lid on the pan simmer for 30 minutes. Clean the stomach and check carefully for thin patches, for these will cause the stomach to burst during cooking.

Chop up the heart, lungs and liver finely, if you like you can rub half of the liver into a pulp. Now mix all the ingredients except the stomach and fill ⅔ of the stomach with this mixture. The contents will swell during cooking, so leave a little space for this. Push the air from the stomach and carefully tie it up at the top. Put the stomach in a pan, cover completely with water and simmer gently for 3 hours. Prick a few holes in the stomach with a needle when it starts swelling—this prevents bursting.

Variation use the sheep's kidneys and tongue instead of the lungs. Or make the haggis from lamb's organs.

Head cheese

Put pieces of pig's head or calf's head (washed) in salted water, bring to the boil and simmer for 15 minutes. Then throw away the water and put them in a pan with stock. Leave to simmer until the meat comes away from the bone.

Take the pieces of head from the stock and boil the liquid down a bit longer. Meanwhile bone the head completely and chop up the meat. Sieve the stock.

Mix the chopped meat with garden herbs, chopped up onions, salt, pepper, pressed garlic and spoonfuls of the reduced liquid. Put everything in a pastry mould and let it set in the fridge.

Variation add a little vinegar to the stock and stir a few stuffed olives through the chopped mixture. Serve this head cheese with vinaigrette.

Rillettes de porc

500 gm (1¼ lb) streaky pork
some savory
1 clove of garlic
some sage
water
salt
bouquet garni
freshly ground pepper

If necessary, cut the rinds off the fatty edges, and cut the meat into small cubes. Put them in a pan with the herbs and a little water. Now let this simmer very gently for a long time. Add a little water from time to time if necessary. You can add some chopped up bones if you like, so that later the meat juices become jelly-like. When the meat starts falling apart, remove it from the pan, put it in a flat dish and shred it with two forks. Add as much juice as you think necessary, taste it, and finish the mixture with seasoning. Cool, and stir firmly when it starts setting. Then put it in preserving jars and cover them with melted fat. The rillettes can be kept fairly long in a cool place.

Potted meat

'Cut six pounds of rump steak into pieces, spice with mace, pepper, clove and ginger, finely pounded together, and mix with salt; put in a cooking pot with 2 pounds of butter; bake for four hours, well-covered; before it gets cold take out the meat, finely pound it and press it into jars, and pour over the clarified butter.'

This is a recipe from *The Country Housewife*, 1753, written by Richard Bradley.

Poultry and Game Recipes

Game and poultry are very popular as the main ingredient of terrines, pâtés, galantines and the like. Wherever people hunted and poached—and still do—pâtés are prepared. It is a festive way to make a sumptuous dish out of unsightly pieces of edible offal. Older animals, which could taste rather tough and bitter when roasted or fried, melt on your tongue when worked into a pâté. And by adding all kinds of other ingredients, more people can enjoy the delicious flavour of game and poultry. A piece of left-over roast game, worked into a terrine, will permeate the whole dish with its powerful aroma. All kinds of extravagant things can be done with poultry pâtés. If, for instance, you have been given a pheasant, keep the head and tail in the fridge or deep-freeze. Make a pâté in the shape of the body and at the last moment attach the head and tail. Let the feathers hang luxuriantly over the edge of the dish and serve the pâté in this way.

People used to make pâtés in the shape of large birds and sometimes these were brought in, spitting fire. Or people used to put a pig's head on top of the pâté, poured in brandy, and set fire to it.

The English used to have a very nice pie, the *umble pie*, made from edible intestines and offal of the deer. *Umbles* means edible insides and is not derived from the word *humble*, as many people think. In *David Copperfield*, by Charles Dickens, someone said: 'I ate umble pie with an appetite', but this was probably someone who dropped his h's, like so many Londoners. *To eat humble pie* means to make an apology, or to submit to humiliation. The umble pie later took on the meaning of a simple pâté prepared with all kinds of offal. The animals most used in pâtés are goose (especially the liver), duck, pigeon, pheasant, partridge, chicken, rabbit, hare and roe deer.

Pâtés and Pastries

The same rules and guidelines apply for poultry and game pâtés as for meat pâtés. Be a little more sparing with salt, and adjust the herbs and spices. Let the prime pieces marinate in a little cognac or other drink and put them in layers between the filling.

Pâté maison with game or poultry (basic recipe)

See basic recipe for Pâté maison, under Meat recipes. Use 400 gm (1 lb) of left-over bits of poultry or game meat instead of the 400 gm (1 lb) of lean meat, and use chicken-liver or similar instead of pig's liver. Cooked left-overs are also very suitable.

Or use the recipe *Pâté Marry* and substitute prime pieces of back, breast or leg of poultry or game for the fillet of pork. Replace the smoked bacon by fresh fatty bacon and fill out the mixture's lean meat with bits of offal from the poultry or game such as liver and heart.

Pâté de Chartres en croûte (chicken)

Use a pastry dough or shortcrust pastry. For the filling:

1 chicken with liver and heart
400 gm (1 lb) lean pork
400 gm (1 lb) belly pork without rind
2 tblsp port
a few strips of fresh fatty bacon
3 eggs
1 cup cream
some quatre épices
salt

Cut the chicken into pieces and fry them briefly. Take all the meat off the bones, keep a few prime pieces, like breast and leg, separate, and marinate them in port for some time.

Mince or chop up the rest of the chicken together with the liver, the heart and the pork, and season with herbs. Leave the filling for a few hours. Add the marinade and taste.

Line a greased baking tin with ⅔ of the rolled-out dough. Lay a few slices of bacon on the bottom, a layer of filling and a layer of marinated chicken on top. Continue this way and finish up with a layer of filling. Put a few slices of bacon on top and attach the lid to the pâté. Make a chimney in the lid, decorate with bits of pastry if you like, and coat the pastry with beaten egg, egg white or a little milk. Bake the pâté in a pre-heated oven at 180–200°C (360–400°F) for about 1½ hours. The pâté is done if a knife, stuck in through the chimney, comes out clean.

Variation use another kind of bird or game instead of chicken.

Chicken pie

wholemeal pastry or shortcrust pastry

1 roasting chicken
150 gm (6 oz) boiled ham
200 gm (8 oz) minced pork
1 finely chopped small onion
100 gm (4 oz) mushrooms, sliced
1 small glass white wine or madeira
or dry white vermouth or cider
salt and freshly ground pepper
100 gm (4 oz) fresh fatty bacon
1 clove garlic, pressed
1 tsp marjoram or tarragon
or sage or another fresh herb
1 tblsp parsley
2 eggs (optional) and either
some cream and flour, or some tomato purée

Follow the same procedure described in the previous recipe. If you like, pour a little chicken jelly through the chimney when the pâté is cool.

Variation use rabbit, turkey, goose or another animal instead of the chicken.

Pâté de canard d'Amiens

This is an old method used centuries ago to prepare this duck, the difference being that now, as opposed to former times, the duck is boned. This not only makes it a lot simpler to prepare, but also to eat. Ask your poulterer to bone the duck for you, or do it yourself with a small, sharp, pointed knife, and start by cutting open the back.

Make a pastry dough, shortcrust pastry or hot water crust pastry.

1 duck with liver and heart
1 goose liver or 100 gm (1¼ lb) chicken livers
400 gm (1 lb) belly pork
200 gm (8 oz) rabbit or veal
200 gm (8 oz) lean pork
½ cup strong stock
½ cup madeira
½ cup calvados or cognac
2 eggs
salt and freshly ground pepper
some truffle cuttings (optional)
some thyme
some ground bay
some allspice (optional)
100 gm (4 oz) edible fungi
a few rashers fresh fatty bacon or egg-white

Marinate a few cubes of duck meat, which you have cut off the plumpest parts of the duck, in 2 tablespoons of calvados or cognac, a little allspice or thyme and pepper. For the filling chop the fungi up finely and fry them briefly in a little butter. Then finely chop the livers, the pork, rabbit, the heart and, if you use them, the truffles, and mix them together. Put the calvados in a saucepan, heat it, set it alight and pour it over the meat mixture. Add the stock madeira, fungi, eggs, spices, herbs and marinade liquid. Make a purée of the mixture in an electric blender and put it three times through the finest blade of a mincer. Stir in the duck cubes. Taste.

Fill the duck with ⅓ of this filling and sew it up. Sometimes the duck is briefly fried on all sides in a little oil, but this is not necessary. Now line a large greased terrine or baking mould with ⅔ of the pastry. Coat the pastry with a little egg white or put very thin slices of bacon on the bottom. Put a layer of filling on top and then the stuffed duck. Now fill the terrine with more filling, on top of the duck, cover with bacon, if you like, and attach the pastry lid to the pâté. Make a little hole in the middle of the lid, decorate it with left-over bits of pastry, and coat the lid with a little beaten egg. Bake the pâté in a pre-heated oven at 175–200°C (350–400°F) for 1½ hours or more. Make a nice jelly from the duck's carcass and a few pig's bones, with madeira, and the following day pour it through the hole onto the pâté.

The pâté can be baked just as well without a terrine. Make 2 oval-shaped pieces of pastry, larger than the duck. Put one piece on a greased baking tin, cover it with half of the filling (leave an edge all round) and put the duck on top. Completely cover the duck with the rest of the filling, put the other piece of pastry on top and press the edges firmly together. Make a little chimney in the lid, decorate with left-over bits of pastry and coat with beaten egg.

This pâté can be made with any other bird.

For a *pâté de bécasses* use 4 woodcocks instead of the duck and leave out the allspice, add a little parsley and use armagnac instead of calvados. Add a clove of garlic and/or a few shallots or mix in some grapes. Thus you can also make *thrush pâté, pigeon pâté, guinea-fowl pâté, fowl pâté, partridge pâté, pheasant pâté* or whatever.

Lombardian chicken patties

Pâtés à la mode Lombarde were described as early as 1393 by *Le Ménagier de Paris*, and Messisbugo, too, gives recipes for it in 1556 in his *Libro Nove nel qual s'insegna a far ogni sorti di vivanda*.

In those days people usually used a whole chicken, but it works just as well with breast of chicken. A thick slice of rolled turkey is also nice. Use flaky or shortcrust pastry.

4 boned chicken breasts (fillet)
1 beaten egg
1 tblsp lemon juice
4 thin rashers of bacon
a little ginger powder
pinch of cinnamon
pinch of clove
pinch of cardamom

Mix the egg with the lemon juice and the herbs, add some breadcrumbs (optional) and some chopped parsley, and toss the chicken pieces in this mixture.

Roll out the pastry and make it into 4 round pieces. Put a rasher of bacon on top of each piece of pastry and a chicken piece on top of it. When you have made the egg mixture, pour a few drops on top and seal the pastry. Spread a little beaten egg over the patties. Bake them in a pre-heated oven at 200–225°C (400–440°F) for about 20–30 minutes until golden brown. Shortcrust pastry should be baked in a slightly cooler oven 175°C (350°F) for a little longer.

Rabbit pâté

Wild rabbits are the nicest, but you can also make this with tame ones.

1 wild or tame rabbit
salt and freshly ground pepper
75 gm (3 oz) bacon fat
500 gm (1¼ lb) minced pork or half pork mince and half beef mince
200 gm (8 oz) liver or lean veal
1 clove garlic
1 onion
1½ cups rosé or white wine
2 tblsp marc or cognac
2 eggs
2 tblsp flour
a lot of thyme
salt and freshly ground pepper
shortcrust pastry

Divide the rabbit into 4 pieces, sprinkle them with salt, pepper and thyme and fry them in bacon fat on a moderate heat for no longer than half an hour. While the rabbit is cooling, make the pastry, and put it in the fridge.

Cut the meat off the bone and, if you like, keep a few of the best pieces aside, like the back and the leg. Chop up the rest of the meat finely, as well as the liver or veal, the onion and the garlic. You can also put it through the mincer and mix it with the rosé, the marc in which you have dissolved the flour; the eggs and the herbs. Leave the filling for a number of hours, taste and season. Line a greased terrine mould or baking tin with ⅔ of the rolled out pastry and put in the filling and the pieces of rabbit, layer by layer. Start and finish with filling. Cover the pâté with the rest of the pastry, prick a few holes in the lid or make a chimney and coat the pâté with beaten egg. Place it in the centre of a pre-heated oven at about 175°C (350°F) and bake for just under an hour. Serve the pâté hot, or pour a little jelly into it to serve it cold.

Variation Mix some mushrooms and/or truffle cuttings through the filling. Or leave out the rosé, and use 1 tablespoon of lemon juice with 1 tablespoon of parsley. Or use red wine instead of rosé, with less thyme and a few juniper berries and rosemary. Or just work some port into the filling.

Hare pâté, venison pâté, and other kinds of **game pâté** are made in the same way. Start off with 500–750 gm (1¼–1¾ lb) of game meat. If you like, you can mix some truffles and pistachio nuts through the filling. Or put a layer of cowberry-compôte on top.

Pâté de foie gras de Strasbourg

You could, of course, simply buy a tin of this, put the pâté in a home-made pastry (or brioche dough), bake it and serve it hot or cold. That is the simplest way. But here is the official recipe for an authentic enlarged goose liver. The pâté can also be prepared with ordinary goose livers and duck livers.

pastry
1 goose liver of about 500 gm (1¼ lb)
300 gm (12 oz) fresh fatty bacon
300 gm (12 oz) pork
⅓ cup cognac
salt and freshly ground pepper
herbs, (parsley, thyme and bayleaf)
150 gm (6 oz) lean veal
150 gm (6 oz) calf's liver
⅓ cup madeira
3 or 4 truffles or some cuttings

Clean the liver, cut off all the green-coloured parts as well as the connective tissue. Let it marinate for 24 hours in the cognac, madeira, truffles, salt, pepper and herbs. Cut the fatty bacon into cubes and let these melt a little in a frying pan. Meanwhile cut the calf's liver, the pork and the veal into small cubes and pour the fat from the bacon over them. Remove the rest of the bacon from the pan, put in the cubed meat with the fat, and fry briefly on a high heat without browning. Take the pan from the heat, add the bacon cubes and let everything cool off. Put the mixture through a mincer, pound it finely in a mortar and sieve it. Add the marinade liquid from the goose liver and mix well. Taste. Line a pie dish or baking tin with the pastry and put a layer of filling on the bottom and round the sides. Poke pieces of filling into the goose liver and lay it on the filling. Cover completely with the rest of the filling, put the pastry on top, make a chimney in it and coat the pâté with beaten egg. Bake it in a fairly hot oven for about 45–60 minutes. When the pâté is completely cool, or on the day it will be served, pour some jelly into it.

Carême made a *pâté chaud de foie gras aux truffes* with two different fillings of goose liver. One with goose liver, bacon fat, shallots, mushrooms, truffles, parsley, herbs and spices. The other with goose liver, scallops, egg yolks and truffles. Both were puréed and baked in layers, in a crust. Towards the end of the baking time some sherry was poured into the pâté.

Terrines

Chicken liver terrine

500 gm (1¼ lb) chicken livers
milk
1–2 cloves of garlic
2 tblsp cognac or other drink
some tarragon
a pinch of nutmeg
salt and freshly ground pepper
4 eggs
1½ cups cream
4 tblsp flour

Cut off the unwanted parts of the livers and soak them in milk for a few hours. Drain and make a purée of them, in an electric mixer. Beat the eggs, press the garlic, dissolve the flour in the cognac and mix it with the other ingredients. Let the mixture stand for a while and taste. Butter an oven-proof dish or pie dish and spoon in the mixture. Cover the dish with foil and cook the terrine *au-bain-marie* in a preheated oven at 150–175°C (324–350°F) for about 1½ hours.

Variation Use some cloves and parsley instead of the tarragon and nutmeg. If you like, leave out the eggs and flour. Or mix in green pepper. Or leave the pepper out of the above recipe and sprinkle bruised peppercorns on the filling before you bake it, and you have a *terrine de foie de volaille aux poivres noirs*.

A very special effect is produced by mixing some anchovy paste and 250 gm (10 oz) minced pork through the filling in the above recipe, leaving out the tarragon and nutmeg and mixing in a finely chopped onion and some ground cloves. Then you have a *Danish chicken-liver pâté*.

Livering Puddings from the time of Elizabeth I of England are described in *The Good Housewive's treasury* of 1588: leave out the garlic, cream, flour, cognac and tarragon and add 1 tablespoonful of chicken fat, some breadcrumbs and 2 tablespoonfuls of raisins.

Chicken-liver pâté

500 gm (1¼ lb) chicken livers
milk
75 gm (3 oz) butter, or in part, chicken fat
1 chopped onion
1 clove garlic
salt and freshly ground pepper
cayenne pepper
4 tblsp white wine
2 tblsp cognac
1 tsp fresh marjoram
1 tsp basil or rosemary
⅔ cup cream

Wash the chicken-livers, put them in some milk for an hour and drain them well. Fry the onion and the finely sliced garlic in ⅔ of the butter, add the chicken-livers and bake for 5 minutes. Remove the livers from the pan, add the herbs and quench with the wine and cognac. Take the pan from the heat and add the liquid to the livers. Purée the livers in an electric mixer or rub them through a sieve. Stir in the rest of the butter and the cream and season to taste. Fill a terrine with the mixture and put a few sprigs of parsley, almonds, etc. on top. Cover the pâté and let it stiffen in the fridge for at least 12 hours.

Variation leave out the fresh herbs, add some nutmeg and a chopped-up boiled egg and you have a *Russian chicken-liver terrine.*

Gateau de foie de volaille au Coulis de crevettes

Make this chicken-liver terrine with a shrimp sauce just before serving.

200 gm (8 oz) chicken-livers
50 gm (2 oz) bone marrow
2 tblsp concentrated jelly or meat gravy
salt and freshly ground pepper
½ cup milk or coffee cream
2 eggs
2 egg yolks
½ clove garlic

Rub the ingredients through a sieve or purée them in an electric mixer. You should be left with a thick cream. Put the purée in a buttered ovenproof dish: do not fill it too full as the mixture will rise. Cover the dish with aluminium foil and tie it firmly. Set the dish on a grill in a panful of cold water, which should reach at least half-way up the dish. Slowly bring the water almost to boiling point and keep it there for about 1½ hours. Meanwhile make a sauce of:

100 gm (4 oz) shrimps
2 egg yolks
75 gm (3 oz) soft butter
100 gm (4 oz) finely sliced mushrooms, briefly fried in butter
⅔ cup whipping cream

Stir the shrimps, butter, cream and egg yolks together *au-bain-marie* to make a sauce. Stir occasionally. At the very last moment add the mushrooms and pour the sauce over the chicken-liver terrine, which has been turned on to a hot serving dish.

Turkey terrine

This dish is an excellent way to use up turkey left-overs after Christmas. Do not eat the terrine until 2–3 weeks after preparation so that your memories of the lavish Christmas dinner have faded somewhat.

200 gm (8 oz) cold, minced turkey
the turkey's liver
125 gm (5 oz) calf's or pig's liver
125 gm (5 oz) ground pork
1 clove garlic, pressed
2 tblsp cognac

125 gm (5 oz) thin slices of fresh fatty bacon
freshly ground black pepper
1 tsp salt
2 sprigs chopped parsley or
some thyme or marjoram
60 gm (2½ oz) soft butter

Mix all the ingredients thoroughly, except the bacon, and leave the mixture for a few hours. Taste and place in a terrine which has been lined with bacon, cover with bacon and then the lid. Bake the terrine for about 1½ hours *au-bain-marie* in a preheated oven at 150–175°C (325—350°F). Do not open the terrine until it is completely cool; if you like, seal it with melted fat.

   Terrine of Pigeon or other birds are prepared in the same way.

Dutch hare terrine

1 hare
vinegar or red wine
500 gm (1¼ lb) lean calf's liver
500 gm (1¼ lb) lean pork
500 gm (1¼ lb) fresh fatty bacon
25 gm (1 oz) salt
2 tsp pepper
2 tsp nutmeg
4 chopped shallots
1 glass madeira
5 egg yolks

Marinate the hare in red wine or vinegar for 48 hours. Cut the meat off the bones and keep the best pieces separate. Mince the rest of the hare, veal and pork, with the bacon left over after lining the pie dishes.

   Mix the remaining ingredients, leave for a while then taste. Put the filling and slices of hare in the pie dishes, layer by layer. Lay a few slices of bacon on top and put on the lids. Seal with some rye flour and water. Bake the terrines in a moderate oven *au-bain-marie* for about 2 hours. Do not remove the lids until the terrines are cold and then pour a thin coat of molten lard over them. Well-covered and unopened, the terrine will keep for a few months.

Variation add 2 cloves of garlic with some thyme, bay and mace instead of the nutmeg, some cognac and red wine instead of the madeira, and add some grated orange rind or lemon rind.

Pies and Flans

Pigeon pie (by Gouffé)

'Prepare oysters of fillet steak and four pigeons cut in half. Remove the breast bones. Season them with salt and pepper. Put the steak oysters on the bottom of the dish and place the pigeon halves on top until the dish is full; also add six hard-boiled eggs.

Pour over a sauce Espagnole and finish it off like a steak pie.' This pie was supposed to be baked first in a suet pastry crust and a strong pigeon stock, then the crust was broken and pushed inside the pie which was then covered with flaky pastry and baked further. Nowadays, onions, garlic, wine, port, mushrooms and bacon are often added.

Venison pie

This pie can also be baked in the form of small patties. It is usually garnished with water-cress.

1 cup red wine
hot-water crust pastry or flaky pastry
strong game or beef stock
1 kg (2¼ lb) breast or shoulder of venison, or other game
50 gm (2 oz) chopped onion
1 tblsp flour
flour mixed with salt pepper and mace
redcurrants or rowan berries
75 gm (3 oz) butter

Cut the venison into pieces, toss them in the flour and fry them briefly in half of the butter. Add the wine and as much stock as needed to cover the meat. Add the onion and simmer gently until the meat is done. Pour off the gravy and use with the rest of the butter and the flour, to make a sauce, and season to taste. Put the venison and the sauce in an ovenproof dish. Cover the dish with pastry, make a chimney in the lid and coat it with egg. Bake the pie in a preheated oven at 200°C (400°F) if you have used hot-water crust pastry and 250°C (480°F) if you have used flaky pastry, until done. Finally, pour some redcurrant jelly through the chimney.

Batalia pie

'Take four small chickens and young doves, four sucking-rabbits, cut them into pieces and season with aromatic herbs; lay them in a pie with four sweetbreads cut into slices, an equal amount of sheep's tongues and battered palates, two pairs of lambstones (kidneys), twenty or thirty large mushrooms; put butter on top and seal the pâté with a layer.'

This pie was very popular in England in the 17th and 18th centuries. It was based on the French recipe *Béatailles*, which also used artichoke hearts and mushrooms. This recipe comes from *The Country Housewife*, 1753, by Richard Bradley, like this *Swan-pye*: 'skin and bone the swan, lard it with bacon and season it with aromatic herbs and a few powdered bay leaves; put butter on top and seal the pie.'

Bstilla (Moroccan chicken pie)

2 chickens or 1 large fowl with heart and liver
7–8 eggs
150 gm (6 oz) butter
1 large, finely-chopped onion
salt and black pepper
1 heaped tsp ground ginger
½ tsp saffron
1 heaped tsp quatre épices
3 tblsp finely chopped parsley
some water or stock
1 tblsp sugar
some cinnamon
150 gm (6 oz) chopped, roasted almonds
1 beaten egg yolk
flaky pastry

Cut each chicken into four pieces, fry them in the butter, add onion, spices and parsley and some water or stock. Simmer until the meat falls off the bone. Let the heart and the liver simmer in this mixture for a while, too. Remove the chicken from the pan, skin and bone and cut it into small pieces. Take a cupful of the cooking liquid, beat it with the eggs, let it thicken on a low heat and season to taste. Line a greased flan mould with a thin layer of pastry, put the almonds, the sugar, the cinnamon and half of the sauce on top. Cover with another thin layer of pastry and put the chicken with the rest of the egg mixture on top. Sprinkle some stock over the layers of filling, if you like, and seal the pie with pastry. Spread the egg yolk over the pastry. Bake for 30–40 minutes in an oven at 175°C (350°F) and then 15 minutes at 225–250°C (440–480°F).

Sundries

Chicken galantine

The following recipe is the basic method for all poultry. Vary the amount of filling for small birds or use a number of them. Turkey, goose, guinea-fowl, large pheasant and pigeons are usually worked into this dish for parties and celebrations, but rabbit, hare or roe deer are also suitable.

Take a large free range chicken and ask your poulterer to bone it for you. Extract a potent stock from the carcass, using half a bottle of wine and the ingredients of the basic recipe for stock.

Then make a filling with:

500 gm (1¼ lb) lean meat (pork, pork and veal, or chicken and veal, etc.)
400 gm (1 lb) fresh fatty back bacon
100 gm (4 oz)
2 eggs
liver and heart of the chicken
sel épicé or herbs, spices and salt to taste

Mince the meat as finely as possible and make a purée of it. Mix the ingredients thoroughly, season to taste, let the mixture rest for a while and taste.

To make a salpicon you can use:

prime pieces cut from the fleshy parts of the chicken
truffle cuttings
goose liver or other livers
blanched pistachio nuts
100 gm (4 oz) boiled tongue
cognac or other drink for marinating
100 gm (4 oz) fatty ham or fresh fatty bacon

If you want to mix the salpicon through the filling, cut everything into cubes. Let these marinate in the cognac. Place the chicken with the skin underneath on a clean cloth and place some meat from the thick parts on the parts that are too thin. Sprinkle some salt and pepper over it. Spread the filling over the top, or put on half the filling, then a layer of salpicon and another layer of filling. Now bring the edges of the skin together and sew up the chicken. Firmly wrap it in the cloth (usually cheesecloth) and tie the ends together securely.

The stock should have simmered for at least 2 hours before you put the chicken in it. Cook the chicken for 2 hours or more in the gently bubbling stock. Remove the pan from the heat and let the chicken cool in the stock for at least another hour. Take the chicken out of the stock and put a fairly heavy weight on it, slightly less than 1 kilo (2 lb), otherwise the galantine will end up too dry. Sieve the stock, boil it down somewhat and season it to taste. Leave the galantine and the stock in the fridge overnight. Scrape the fat from the jelly and, if it is not firm enough, add some gelatine and cool once again. Carefully remove the cloth from the chicken, pull out the thread and put it on a grid. Take some jelly, just fluid enough to spread over the chicken. Let the jelly layer set in the fridge and repeat the process. If you like, you can decorate the chicken by sticking on slices of cucumber, paprika peppers, radishes and the like, with a little jelly, then finish off with another layer of jelly. Lay the galantine on an attractive dish and garnish with chopped jelly.

Poultry mousse

500 gm (1¼ lb) cold poultry
some lemon juice
½ cup cream
a dash of sherry
1 litre (1¾ pints) chicken stock
100 gm (4 oz) cooked poultry livers
6 slices of gelatine

Boil the skimmed stock down to ½ litre, stir in the sherry and lemon juice off the heat, and when the stock has cooled down a bit add the soaked gelatine. Mince the meat and the liver very fine, beat the stiff jelly until frothy and whip the cream. Mix all the ingredients thoroughly, taste and season. Let the mousse set for a while in a mould in the fridge. Turn it out before serving.

Chicken-liver mousse

Leave out the cream from the chicken-liver pâté recipe (p. 81), beat some chicken jelly until frothy, whip 1½ cups of cream until stiff and carefully mix both into the chicken-liver paste. Leave to set for some time in the fridge.

Preserved goose

500 gm (1¼ lb) goose meat, in pieces
500 gm (1¼ lb) pork cutlet, in pieces
50 gm (2 oz) salt
1½ tsp saltpetre
500 gm (1¼ lb) goose fat or fresh fatty bacon
some fresh sage
some fresh thyme
½ tsp mace or other
herbs to taste
pepper

Mix the salt, saltpetre, the spices and herbs together, sprinkle them over the meat and leave overnight. Melt the fat and add the meat. Put a lid on the pan and very slowly simmer the meat until done.

After an hour see if the meat is soft and remove it from the fat. Let it drain. Pour off the clear fat and throw the rest away. Put a layer of fat in a clear glass preserving jar, let it set and put the pieces of meat on top. Put one kind of meat in each pot or make layers of meat. Pour the rest of the fat on top as far as the rim and close the jars. This is a *confit*

d'oie. Instead of the fat you can use 1 cup red wine, leave out the saltpetre, use less salt and let the meat marinate in this. Then cook the meat in layers in an oven dish (securely covered) in the oven. Cool it under a weight and seal the meat with clarified butter. Now it is *potted goose*. Serve these dishes (warmed up if you like) with a piquant sweet-sour sauce. You can do this with all sorts of poultry and game. If you follow the latter method of preparation, add about 75 gm (3 oz) of fat when using a dry sort of meat.

Fish Recipes

'Was never Pyk walwed in galauntyne/As I in love am walwed and y-wounded' said Chaucer in the *Canterbury Tales* about a pike in jelly, but a fish pâté, too, is worthy of such a song of praise. In the east of Holland I once had a seawolf pâté with mousseline sauce—so unforgettably delicious that I still dream about it! Unfortunately fish pâtés are seldom served. If they are kept or warmed up they lose their aroma and I think that these technical difficulties are the reason why they so rarely appear on menus in restaurants.

So, rather than making a fish pâté, terrine or mousse the day before, make it on the day you need it. Never heat up a fish pâté. The delicate aroma will not survive such treatment. Be more careful with herbs, spices, salt and drink than for other pâtés. All kinds of fish and shellfish can be worked into pâtés, terrines and mousses. Dry fish such as whiting, haddock and cod are usually used for the filling. Richer kinds such as salmon, tuna fish and eel are usually sliced and put between the filling, as are shellfish. Fresh fish is preferable by far to frozen fish; never buy already defrosted fish from the deep freeze. Defrost the fish in the fridge just before you are going to use it.

As with other pâtés, use your imagination and experience. For example, if you have liked a particular combination of ingredients in a fish dish you have made, then try this in a fish pâté or mousse.

Pâté and Pastries

Fish for a pâté en croûte or pie is first poached in a court-bouillon, before the pâté en croûte or pie is constructed. This court-bouillon should not be more than luke-warm when you slide the fish into it, if it is too hot the fish will fall apart more quickly. The court-bouillon should never boil and 80°C (175°F) is sufficient to solidify the fish's protein. The flavour is also preserved better. If you do not prepare the fish and the stock immediately, then let the fish cool in the liquid. It benefits both the fish and the stock.

Fish pâté maison

500 gm (1¼ lb) fish (haddock, cod, devil fish, seawolf, gurnard or the like)
100 gm (4 oz) peeled shrimps or mussels
1 pint court-bouillon (see Recipes for pastry, stock and jelly)
a little white wine
flaky pastry, shortcrust pastry or sour cream pastry
some garlic, parsley and breadcrumbs (optional)
4 tblsp butter
4 tblsp flour
4 tblsp cream or sour cream
2 tblsp cognac or other drink
salt and freshly ground pepper
a few fresh herbs to taste
2 eggs
some lemon juice and/or grated cheese (optional)

Poach the fish in the court-bouillon with a little wine for no longer than 5 minutes, and let them cool together. Take the fish out of the liquid and, if necessary, remove the skins and bones. Reserve the best pieces, (about ¼ of the total), and mash the rest with a fork. If you are going to peel the shrimps yourself add the shells to the court-bouillon and boil them for 10 minutes, this gives the pâté a very special flavour. Or mix in a little juice from the mussels.

Now make a thick sauce by melting the butter in a pan, adding the flour off the heat, frying it for a while and adding some sieved fish stock. Add the cream and the cognac and, if necessary, some more stock. Season the sauce with salt, pepper, herbs and (optional) some lemon juice, garlic or grated cheese. Remove the pan from the heat and, when the sauce has cooled a little, stir in the eggs and the mashed fish. Taste again.

Roll out the dough and line a greased cake tin with ⅔ of the pastry. If you like, you can sprinkle on the bottom a mixture of parsley and breadcrumbs, briefly fried together in a little butter. Then pour half of the sauce into the mould, put the pieces of fish and the shrimps on top and cover them with the rest of the sauce. Put the pastry lid on the pâté, prick a pattern of holes into it or make a chimney. Decorate it if you wish with left-over bits of pastry and coat the lid with milk, egg white, yolk or a little butter. Put the pâté in the fridge until 1½ hours before serving it. Pre-heat the oven to 200–225°C (400–

440°F), place the pâté in the centre of the oven and after 15 minutes reduce the heat to 175°C (350°F) or 10 minutes in an electric oven. The total baking time is about 45 minutes, depending on the depth of the pâté. Stick a knitting needle or a knife through the chimney and if it comes out completely clean, the pâté is done. Let it cool for another 10 minutes before you take it from the mould and serve it.

Variation place a layer of drained and cooked spinach in the pâté, and you have a *Florentine pâté*. Or colour the filling pink with a little tomato purée and then give the pâté the grand name of *Pâté de poisson Aurora*. A few blanched almonds, pistachio nuts or mushrooms are also very nice in the filling.

Pâté with Scallops

Instead of 500 gm (1¼ lb) of fish in the previous recipe use 400 gm (1 lb) of fish for the filling alone and a good 100 gm (4 oz) of poached scallops; and substitute mushrooms for the shrimps. If you can buy fresh scallops in winter, then buy a kilo (2 lbs). Open them, take out the muscle from the shell, remove the slime and dark parts and leave the orange bit. Rinse them thoroughly until clean and poach for 5 minutes in court-bouillon or water. Use the poach-liquid or the liquid from tinned scallops for the sauce. Follow the same method as described above.

Tuna fish pâté

See the recipe for *Fish pâté maison*, but use 400 gm (1 lb) of fish instead of 500 gm (1¼ lb) and work it completely into the filling. Substitute 200 gm (8 oz) of tuna for the shrimps; fresh tuna fish is definitely nicer than tinned, although you can use tinned. If you use smoked or fresh mackerel instead of the tuna, you will have a *mackerel pâté*. *Crab pâté, eel pâté, salmon pâté, trout pâté with almonds, oyster pâté*, or whatever fish pâté you can think of, are all made in the same way. Do adjust the flavour of the filling though—a smoked fish can take a stronger filling than a trout for instance.

Feuilleté de saumon frais (fresh salmon pâté)

flaky pastry
500 gm (1¼ lb) fresh salmon
5 cups boiled rice
court-bouillon with salt
5 hardboiled sliced eggs
1 cup finely chopped fresh herbs
(parsley, chives, chervil)
100 gm (4 oz) butter
2 tblsp lemon juice

Poach the salmon in the court-bouillon for 5 minutes and let them cool together. Take the salmon out, skin it, discard the bones and cut it into strips. Melt the butter and stir it through the rice. Roll out the pastry into two equal rectangles and place one in a greased baking tin. Sprinkle half of the herbs over it and put half of the rice on top. Then a layer with half of the egg slices and all the salmon. Add salt and freshly ground pepper and sprinkle with lemon juice. Next put in the rest of the egg, the rice and the garden herbs and cover everything with the other piece of pastry. Spread egg white or water over the edges, press them firmly together, make a chimney in the highest point and coat the pâté with beaten egg. Bake it in a pre-heated oven at 225–250°C (440–480°F) for 45 minutes.

Serve the pâté hot, with a sauce made from:

1 cup cream
juice of 1½ lemons
salt
freshly ground pepper

Stir these ingredients together and carefully heat the mixture, it must definitely not boil.

Fish flan (Tart of fysshe)

The following two recipes are from *The Forme of Cury*, of about 1390, written by the head chefs of King Richard II. Proportions were never given in medieval recipes—these are my doing, as well as the description of the first recipe.

400 gm (1 lb) eel or fish fillet

400 gm (1 lb) salmon
100 gm (4 oz) ground almonds
verjuice (cider vinegar with a little sugar or lemon juice can be used)
some nutmeg, ginger and cinnamon
salt and a little sugar
1 slice of toast
enough pastry for an open pie (flaky pastry or wholemeal pastry)

Put 2 heaped tablespoons of almonds, the verjuice and a little salt in a pan with enough water to enable you to poach the fish. Let the liquid boil for 5 minutes and then cool it off. Poach the fish in the liquid for 5 minutes. If you have fish fillets then just poach the salmon. Take the fish from the liquid, clean it and mince or mash it. Take 2 cups of the poaching liquid and add the rest of the almonds. Mix ⅔ cup of this with the salmon and the crushed toast (packet breadcrumbs will also do), the spices, sugar and, if necessary, a little salt. Taste and season. Pepper was much more expensive in those days, and was therefore not used, but you can add some.

Roll out the pastry and line a greased cake tin with it. Make rings from the fish fillet or the eel, cut into strips, put them on the pastry and fill the holes in the rings with half of the salmon paste. Mix the rest of the paste with the almond milk and pour it over the pie. If you like, you can cover it with a pastry lid. Bake it in the oven for about 45 minutes.

Variation mix an egg or egg yolk through the

filling. Or roast some almonds and put a layer of these on the bottom of the dough. Or put some shrimps, mussels, inkfish and the like between the fillets.

Fish pie with herbs (Crustard of eerbis)

'Take good herbs (parsley with a little thyme, lemon balm and rosemary for instance) and finely grind them with the cleaned walnuts (or hazelnuts), a large portion; dilute it with an almost equal amount of verjuice (lemon juice or cider vinegar with a little sugar) and water (boiled for 5 minutes); permeate with powder (this means spices, for instance cinnamon, ginger and pepper) and saffron without salt (salted fish was probably used, but fresh fish is nicer; so do use some salt); make a crust in a mould and put the fish in it, uncooked with a little oil and good powders (spices); when it is half baked add the sauce and bake until done.'

Terrines

The preceding fish pâtés and pies can be baked as terrines. Do not poach the fish first, but mince it raw and stir it through the sauce. Put raw pieces of fish between the filling and put *everything* in a buttered ovenproof dish. Bake the terrine *au-bain-marie* for 1 to 1½ hours, until done.

Green terrine with eel, Brabant style

Briefly steam 500 gm (1¼ lb) of skinned eel, cut into pieces, in a terrine with a little butter. Then add a fair amount of fresh chopped sorrel, spinach, chervil, parsley, sage and savory. Or sorrel, chervil, parsley, chives, sage and savory.

Dilute with 1 cup of beer or white wine and enough water to cover the fish. Season with salt, pepper and thyme. Boil for another 20–25 minutes. Mix 1 or 2 egg yolks with the juice of half a lemon and 1½ tsp of cornflour or potato flour. While stirring, add a little cooking liquid and then stir the egg mixture through the eel sauce. Let it thicken, but not boil. Arrange the pieces of eel in a terrine, pour the sauce over and cool. Serve warm or cold.

Light fish terrine

400–500 gm (1–1¼ lb) fish
1½ cups cream
2 egg whites plus two egg yolks
salt and freshly ground pepper
2 tsp cornflour, dissolved in a little white wine or cognac
herbs to taste, for instance nutmeg, thyme and savory

Beat the egg whites until stiff. Mash the fish and mix it with the other ingredients. This is best done in a blender. Spoon in the egg whites and taste. Put the paste in a buttered ovenproof dish and bake the fish terrine in the oven *au-bain-marie* for about an hour. Serve with a shrimp sauce with dill.

Variation Do not beat the egg whites, but simply mix them through the paste. Also mix in some chopped parsley. Or garden cress. If you leave out either the yolks or the herbs, and use sweet rice wine or sherry instead of white wine and mix in soaked seaweed, you will have a *Japanese fish terrine*.

Cod terrine

500 gm (1¼ lb) cod fillet without bones
50 gm (2 oz) butter
5 tblsp sour cream
1 egg yolk
4 tblsp sherry
1 tblsp lemon juice
2 large boiled potatoes
1 finely chopped onion or 2 shallots
1 pressed clove of garlic
some tabasco or Worcester sauce
1 tblsp chopped parsley
salt and pepper
some tomato purée

Mash the cod and the potatoes, mix all the ingredients together and season. Put the mixture in a buttered terrine and bake it *au-bain-marie* in the oven until done (40–60 minutes).

Variation put the pieces of fish in layers between the mixture.

Mousses and Puddings

Salmon mousse

400–500 gm (1–1¼ lb) poached salmon
1 cup fish jelly
juice of ½ lemon
⅔ cup mayonnaise
250 gm (10 oz) soft cheese; Gervais, Boursin
or Mon Chou
1 tblsp chopped parsley
1 tblsp chopped chives
1 tsp chopped tarragon
some chopped nuts
salt and cayenne pepper (optional)

Tinned salmon is very suitable for this dish.
Mash the salmon and the cheese, make the
fish jelly fluid but not warm and mix all the
ingredients thoroughly. You could, to be on
the safe side, add another 1 or 2 slices of
soaked gelatine to the fish jelly, depending on
the weather (in warm weather the mousse will
'melt' very quickly). Or use 1 cup of water and
4 slices of gelatine instead of the jelly. Let the
mash set in an oiled mould, in the fridge.
Garnish with cucumber slices.

Crab mousse

1 tin of crab, about 250 gm (10 oz)
⅔ cup fish jelly
⅔ cup cream
lemon juice
salt
cayenne pepper
1 tblsp Parmesan cheese
2 egg whites

Mash the crab and the cheese thoroughly,
season with salt, cayenne pepper and lemon
and add the slightly melted jelly. Add the
cream (whipped, if you like). Let the mixture
set a little in the fridge and then spoon in the
stiffly beaten egg whites. Let the mousse set
further and serve it chilled. Instead of the jelly
you can use a pint of water and 3 to 4 slices
of gelatine.

Variation use salmon instead of crab. Or use
sprat for a *sprat mousse*. Substitute Parmesan
cheese for some garlic, use haddock liver
instead of crab and you have a *haddock-liver
mousse*.

Fish pudding with tarragon

500 gm (1¼ lb) fish fillets
3 cups cider
1 bayleaf
1 sprig of thyme
salt and pepper
100–200 gm (4–8 oz) peeled shrimps
6 slices of gelatine
2 very finely chopped shallots
or a pressed clove of garlic
1½ cups whipped cream
1 tblsp finely chopped tarragon
some lemon juice

Poach the fish in the cider with the bayleaf, thyme, salt and pepper. Take the fish from the liquid and let it cool a little. Then add the soaked gelatine and sieve the liquid. Add half of the fish in pieces and the other half mashed, also the shrimps, shallots and tarragon. Let the mash cool completely, stir in the stiffly whipped cream and pour everything into a rinsed-out pudding mould. Let the fish pudding set in the fridge. Turn it out before serving and garnish with tarragon and cucumber for example.

Variation use dill or another herb instead of tarragon. Or use yoghurt instead of the cream and the lemon juice.

Smoked fish-pâté

200 gm (8 oz) smoked fish
150 gm (6 oz) butter
2 tblsp chopped capers
cayenne pepper
2 tblsp chopped parsley
1 tblsp not too dry sherry
1 tblsp lemon juice
salt and pepper
grated nutmeg
a little garlic to taste

Mash the fish very finely and stir all the ingredients together thoroughly. Serve the pâté cooled.

Variation stir a little curd or cottage cheese through the mixture and leave out the butter if you like.

Indonesian shrimp patties

125 gm (5 oz) rice flour
2 eggs
60 gm (2½ oz) melted butter
some salt
some water (optional)

Make a kneadable dough with the above ingredients and roll it out thinly. Cut out round slices or squares. Let it stand for a little while and make the filling.

2 large, finely chopped onions
1–2 finely chopped garlic cloves
1 tblsp coriander
½ tblsp cummin
1 tsp pepper
5 slices chopped ginger
a little turmeric (optional)
some finely chopped sereh
½ tsp brown sugar
1 tsp salt
1 tsp fish paste
250 gm (10 oz) very fine mince
300 gm (12 oz) finely chopped shrimps
a handful of finely cut leeks
1 tblsp chopped parsley
2 djeroek-poeroet leaves
1 tblsp tamarind
some coconut milk

Finely rub the herbs (except the leeks, parsley and djeroek-poeroet) together in a mortar and then fry the mixture in a little oil or butter. Add the mince and the leeks, the parsley and the djeroek-poeroet leaves, fry again for a while and finally add the tamarind and coconut milk. Let it simmer for a while; it should form a thick pulp. Take the pastry slices, put some shrimp mince on each half and spread a little milk or water round the edge. Fold the slices together and press the edges firmly. Coat the patties with a little milk or egg yolk and bake them in the oven or fry them in the oil until they are nice and brown.

Variation use only shrimps.

Egg and Cheese Flans

Quiche Lorraine

flaky pastry
2 rashers smoked bacon
20 gm (1 oz) butter
salt and pepper
4 eggs
1½ cups cream or half cream, half soft cream cheese
a little nutmeg (optional)

Line a greased flan ring with the pastry and prick holes into it with a fork. Beat the eggs and mix them with the cream, salt and pepper. Be careful not to use too much salt, because of the bacon. Cut the bacon into small pieces, fry them in the butter until golden brown and drain them. Put them on the bottom of the flan ring and pour over the egg mixture. Put the quiche immediately in a pre-heated oven at 225°C (440°F). After 20 minutes reduce the heat and bake for another 10 minutes. This is the original recipe, without Gruyère or Parmesan. The very old version of the recipe, with cream cheese, has probably caused the confusion. You could of course mix in 50 gm (2 oz) anyway, but then it is no longer a Quiche Lorraine, but another quiche. The flaky pastry can also be substituted for shortcrust pastry (slightly less rich) and you can mix some nutmeg through the egg mixture. Or mushrooms etc.

Cheese flan

shortcrust pastry or wholemeal pastry
250 gm (10 oz) grated cheese (Gruyère, Parmesan or mature Dutch cheese)
4 eggs
3 cups cream or milk
salt
freshly ground pepper
a little nutmeg

For the preparation see previous recipe, without the bacon.

Variation mix in some mushrooms and bacon or ham, sprinkled with lemon juice and fried briefly in a little butter.

Use less cheese 50–150 gm (2–6 oz), a pinch of garlic (optional), 2 eggs and put a layer of lightly braised vegetables on the bottom: celery for a *celery-cheese flan*, cauliflower for a *cauliflower-cheese flan*, stinging nettles for a *stinging nettle-cheese flan, cabbage-cheese flan, sorrel-cheese flan, artichoke-cheese flan, mushroom-cheese flan, nuts-cheese flan, courgette-cheese flan, potato-cheese flan* with a layer of boiled potatoes, *sauerkraut-cheese flan*—whatever vegetable you can think of, they are all made the same way.

Instead of the vegetable layer you can have a layer of fish or shellfish; a *fish-cheese flan*, or a *scallop-cheese flan*, or a *mussel-cheese flan*, etc.

Add some garlic, paprika, tomato, aubergine, olives, cayenne pepper and, if you like, some shrimps, mussels, pieces of fish and/or inkfish, and you have a *Mediterranean flan*. Or put a thin layer of mince on the bottom: a *cheese-mince flan*. Or add ⅓ cup of white wine, a little garlic and use cream plus Gruyère: a *Swiss cheese flan*.

Greek cheese flan 2 recipes

1
flaky pastry with little butter
450 gm (1 lb 2 oz) Feta cheese or other soft cheese
2 eggs
freshly ground white pepper
4 tblsp mixed fresh herbs
(dill, chervil, chives etc.)

2
flaky pastry with little butter
450 gm (1 lb 2 oz) Feta cheese or other soft cheese
3 eggs and 1 cup yoghurt
freshly ground white pepper
2 finely cut onions, marinated with salt

Beat the cheese, eggs and the other ingredients together thoroughly. Line a greased mould with the pastry, pour in the mixture and bake in a pre-heated oven at 225°C (440°F) for about half an hour. Reduce the heat after 20 minutes.

Tarte de Bry (from *The Forme of Cury*, about 1390)

shortcrust pastry or wholemeal pastry
150 gm (6 oz) Brie, not strong, but a little runny and without crust
3 eggs
some salt
some ginger powder (or pepper)
saffron or turmeric
some sugar (can be left out)

For the preparation see previous recipe. You can pre-bake the pastry crust for 15 minutes, if you like. This is how you make a *Camembert flan*, too.

Gorgonzola flan

pastry of your choice
100 gm (4 oz) Gorgonzola
3 eggs
⅔ cup cream
75 gm (3 oz) Gruyère
pepper and salt

For the preparation see Greek cheese flan. If the Gorgonzola is on the firm side, you can cut it into pieces and stir it through the egg mixture.

A *Roquefort flan* is made with 200 gm (8 oz) of Roquefort, 4 eggs and approximately 1½ cups of cream, depending on the strength of the cheese, without the Gruyère.

Quiche Ardennaise

shortcrust pastry
500 gm (1¼ lb) leeks
a little butter
100 gm (4 oz) Ardenne ham
50 gm (2 oz) Ardenne bacon
2 cups dark beer
2 cups cream
3 egg yolks
2 eggs
fresh parsley
fresh chervil
fresh tarragon
1 finely chopped shallot
salt and freshly ground pepper

Cut the leeks into pieces, throw away only the green leaves with a bluish hue and braise the rest very lightly in butter. Quickly fry the bacon in a dry saucepan. Follow the same method as for a Quiche Lorraine, but first put half of the leeks on the bottom of the pastry, next the ham, the rest of the leeks and then a layer of bacon. Pour the egg mixture over the top. An oven heat of 200°C (400°F) is sufficient.

Tourte Lorraine

shortcrust pastry
200 gm (8 oz) lean pork
200 gm (8 oz) veal
2 glasses white wine
salt and peppercorns
juniper berries and thyme
1 bay leaf
1 clove of garlic
1 shallot, cut into rings
an egg-cream mixture of:
3 eggs
3 cups cream
salt, pepper and nutmeg

Marinate the meat, finely chopped, in the wine and the spices. Line a greased flan ring with ⅔ of the pastry, put the drained meat on top, sprinkle over a little of the marinade and cover with the rest of the pastry. Make a chimney in it. Bake for 40 minutes in a hot oven. Then pour the cream-egg mixture through the chimney and bake for another 15 minutes.

Walnut-cheese flan

wholemeal pastry with lemon rind
25 gm (1 oz) butter
20 gm (¾ oz) flour
1 cup milk
black pepper and cayenne pepper
a little nutmeg or thyme
some garlic (optional)
100–200 gm (4–8 oz) grated Emmenthaler, Gruyère, Parmesan or another cheese
2 egg yolks
2 stiffly beaten egg whites
100 gm (4 oz) chopped walnuts

Line a greased flan ring with the pastry and bake the crust in a hot oven until almost done (15–20 minutes). Meanwhile make a thick béchamel sauce by melting the butter in a small saucepan, adding the flour and, little by little, the milk. Season the sauce with the pepper, the nutmeg (or thyme) and (optional) the garlic. When the sauce has boiled for a while, add the grated cheese. Remove the pan from the heat, stir the beaten egg yolks through the sauce and let it cool. Fold in the stiffly beaten egg whites and the chopped walnuts at the last moment, before you take the flan crust from the oven. Pour the mixture into the crust, grate a little cheese over the top if you like, and put the flan back in the oven. Bake for another 15 minutes until the filling is well-risen and light brown.

Variation substitute part of the milk by white wine and a dash of kirsch.

Cheese flan with sour cream

pastry of your choice
3 eggs
1½ cups sour cream
100–200 gm (4–8 oz) matured cheese, cut
into cubes
a little nutmeg
some oregano or marjoram
a little thyme
a little dill
freshly ground pepper and cayenne pepper

Line a greased flan ring with the pastry and
bake the crust until half done. Beat the eggs
with the sour cream and the herbs. Stir in the
cheese cubes and pour the mixture into the
pastry crust. Or line the bottom of the crust
with the cheese cubes and pour over the egg
mixture. Bake the flan in a fairly hot oven
until done; when a knife is stuck into the
filling and comes out clean, it is done.

Variation substitute half of the sour cream by
milk, use grated cheese instead of cheese
cubes and strew some paprika powder and
chopped parsley over the egg-cheese mixture.
Serve the flan with a chilli-tomato sauce and
you have a *Mexican cheese flan*.

Vegetable recipes

Vegetable pâtés are a boon in our society, where meatless days are a necessity. In old cookery books, too, whole series of recipes for vegetable pâtés can be found, as a change from the fish and egg dishes eaten during fasts, which sometimes lasted a long time. With lentils, soyabeans, brown beans, cereals and the like, delicious tasty dishes can be made, which do not immediately turn out to be winter hot-pots.

Serve vegetable pâtés with a fresh salad and with a nice sauce—a sweet-sour sauce is very suitable.

Mushroom pâté en croûte

wholemeal pastry or pastry with chestnut flour
400 gm (1 lb) mushrooms
4 tblsp chopped parsley
4 tblsp chopped celery
1 finely chopped onion
4 tblsp soft butter
2 beaten eggs
1 carton cottage cheese or curd
30 gm (1 oz) dry breadcrumbs
some basil, finely chopped or powdered
some oregano, finely chopped or powdered
some chopped rosemary
salt and freshly ground pepper
a pinch of cayenne pepper

Put the mushrooms, parsley, celery and onion through a mincer or drum sieve to produce a purée. If you like, briefly fry the onion first. Mix all the ingredients (except the pastry) thoroughly. Taste. Line a sandwich tin with ⅔ of the pastry and spoon in the mixture. Stick the pastry lid on top and bake the pâté for 1–1½ hours until done. Serve hot or cold, garnished with a sprig of parsley.

Toadstool terrine

Use a bag of dried edible fungi (for instance cep) and soak them in water for a few hours. Take all the ingredients of the previous recipe, except the pastry, and add 100 gm (4 oz) of chopped walnuts (other nuts are also possible), 2 tblsp of vermouth and (optional) a clove of garlic. Also purée the walnuts and the soaked fungi. Follow the same method as for the above recipe and use greaseproof paper instead of pastry.

Russian vegetable pâté

sour cream pastry
a small cabbage, white or green
250 gm (10 oz) mushrooms
1 finely chopped onion
4–5 hardboiled eggs
some thyme and marjoram
some tarragon or parsley (optional)
salt and freshly ground pepper
3 tblsp butter
125 gm (5 oz) Mon Chou

Chop up the cabbage, mushrooms and onions. Briefly fry the cabbage and the onions in a frying-pan, add the herbs and stir them in. Remove the vegetables from the pan and briefly fry the mushrooms. Line a greased sandwich-tin with ⅔ of the pastry, put the Mon Chou on the bottom, then a layer of sliced eggs and scatter finely shredded dill over them. Put the cabbage and the onion on top, then the mushrooms and cover the pâté with the rest of the dough. Prick a few holes in the lid, with a fork. Bake the pâté in a pre-heated oven at 200–225°C (400–440°F), after 15 minutes (or 10 minutes in an electric oven) reduce to 175°C (350°F) and bake for another 15–25 minutes until the crust is nice and brown.

Lentil loaf

250 gm (10 oz) lentils
125 gm (5 oz) millet or barley
2 shallots
4 tblsp oil
quite a lot of chopped sorrel or stinging nettles
2 beaten eggs
2 apples, sour-sweet, like pippins
1 tblsp lemon juice
1 tsp ground coriander
salt and pepper to taste
some sunflower seeds

Boil the lentils and the millet or barley until they are just done, do not let them go mushy. Drain them. Chop up the shallots and cut the potatoes into tiny cubes. Briefly fry the shallots in the oil and add the sorrel for one minute. Then mix all the ingredients together, stir well, season and put the mixture in an oiled cake-tin. Bake the loaf in a pre-heated oven until done (about 30–40 minutes).

Variation put a layer of briefly fried mixed vegetables between the lentil mixture. Take, for instance, some cabbage, carrots, leeks and paprika. Or purée the lentils and, if you like, the millet, after they have been boiled, for a *lentil pâté*.

White bean pâté

200 gm (8 oz) white beans
2 chopped shallots
4 tblsp butter
1 chopped onion
2 cloves pressed garlic
1 small grated winter carrot
4 tblsp chopped parsley
2 beaten eggs
30 gm (1 oz) dry breadcrumbs
1 cup cream
salt and freshly ground pepper
coriander and thyme
basil
3 tblsp beer or white wine

Soak the white beans overnight in plenty of water and cook them until soft. Fry the onion, shallots, garlic and carrot. Purée the beans and mix all the ingredients thoroughly. Tip the mixture into an oiled baking-tin and cover with oiled aluminium foil. Bake the pâté in a pre-heated oven at 200–225°C (400–440°F) for about 50-55 minutes, until done. It can be served hot or cold.

Variation substitute tomato purée for beer or use split peas and adjust the herbs.

Artichoke pie from the time of William the Silent

shortcrust pastry
1 tin artichoke hearts or, if you use fresh ones, 4–8 depending on size
2 hardboiled eggs
100 gm (4 oz) white grapes, without pips
2 halved dates without stones
1 glass dry white wine
salt and freshly ground pepper

Line a greased sandwich tin with ⅔ of the dough. Put the sliced eggs on the bottom and on top of that the other ingredients. Fasten the lid on the pâté, coat it with milk and bake the pie in the oven for half an hour. (A béchamel sauce with a little sherry, rather than white wine, seems more suitable to me for this recipe).

Variation use only artichoke hearts for the filling and cover them with an egg-cream mixture of 3 eggs, 1 cup of cream and 125 gm (5 oz) of soft cheese, a little lemon juice, salt and pepper. Strew a little Gruyère over the top, if you like.

Soya bean terrine

600 gm (1½ lb) boiled soya beans
1 small finely chopped onion
1 clove of garlic, pressed
2 finely chopped shallots
4 tblsp butter
4 tblsp flour
1½ cups vegetable stock or milk
1 tsp finely chopped rosemary
1 tsp finely chopped thyme
1 tblsp chopped parsley
4 tblsp wheat germ
2 beaten eggs
salt and pepper

Purée the soya beans. Fry the onion, garlic and shallot and stir them through the soya purée. Melt the butter in a saucepan, stir in the flour, boil for a while and stir in the stock a little at a time, until you have a thick sauce. Let it cool for a while and then stir in the eggs. Now mix all the ingredients together thoroughly. Grease a baking tin with oil, line it well with breadcrumbs and spoon in the mixture. Cover with kitchen foil and bake the terrine in a hot oven at about 200°C (400°F) until done (about half an hour).

Variation add some chopped nuts and cabbage to the mixture and substitute the rosemary for caraway or coriander. Or mix in a little vinegar with honey, this is very nice.

Carrot wholemeal flan

Line a greased flan ring with wholemeal pastry containing oat-flakes. Stir in 5 puréed, cooked winter carrots with 2 tablespoons of tahini (sesame paste), 2 small fried onions, some garlic (optional), herbs (parsley, dill or basil), salt and pepper. Spoon the mixture into the flan and bake it for half an hour in a hot oven, until done.

Leek flan

shortcrust pastry or another kind
1 kg (2¼ lbs) leeks, cut into rings
some butter
3 eggs
1 cup sour cream or cream
⅓ cup sherry
1 tsp dill seed
a little salt
freshly ground pepper

Fry the leeks in some butter until glazed. Mix the beaten eggs with the cream, sherry and herbs. Line a flan ring with ⅔ of the dough, or leave the flan open. Put the leeks on the bottom and pour over the egg mixture. Cover with pastry if you like, and coat with a little egg white. Bake in a hot oven until done (about 45 minutes).

Variation put chicken pieces and boiled tongue under the leeks, with a little parsley, and leave out the dill. Then you have a *chicken and leek pie*. Or, for a flan, put a layer of stiffly beaten egg white on top after 20 minutes of baking, and put the flan back in the oven.

Spinach flan

wholemeal pastry
500 gm (1¼ lb) drained, cooked spinach
3 tblsp dried breadcrumbs
2 tblsp parsley
some butter
2 eggs
2 tblsp cream or sour cream
salt and freshly ground pepper
125 gm (5 oz) bacon, cut into pieces

Line a greased flan ring with the pastry. Briefly fry the breadcrumbs and parsley in some butter and stir in the rest of the ingredients, except the bacon. Spoon the mixture into the ring and put the pieces of bacon on top. Bake the flan in a hot oven until done (30–45 minutes).

Variation add some nutmeg and grated cheese or, if you like, leave out the eggs and the cream, stir 75 gm (3 oz) of butter through the spinach and sprinkle 60 gm (2½ oz) of grated cheese over the top.

The bacon can be left out, as well as the eggs; instead make a béchamel sauce with 2 tablespoons of flour, 2 tablespoons of butter, milk, the cream and 1 egg yolk. If you use asparagus instead of spinach and ham instead of bacon, you have an *asparagus flan*.

What to do with a failed pâté

If, unexpectedly, one day your pâté is a failure (and this could happen to anybody, for you can only call yourself an experienced pâté-maker after some twenty pâtés), do not despair and do not throw the pâté away. There are plenty of things that can be done with it.

A pâté which is too dry

Usually this happens when the pâté has been cooked for too long and is overdone. Or the temperature in the oven was too high; possibly the weight that you put on top while it was cooling was too heavy, or you did not use enough fat.

Stir the meat mixture with a fork, or push it through a sieve and add a little butter or melted bacon fat. Or beat the mixture with some cream, either whipped or not. A little jelly, barely fluid and stirred in, also makes the pâté smoother.

In any case, leave the pâté to set in the fridge for another night.

A pâté which is too bland

You must have used too little salt and too few herbs and not have tasted it often enough. To remedy this, cut the pâté into slices and put slices of cooked salt meat (ham, salted meat or something) between them, sticking the slices together with a little jelly or melted butter.

Or put the pâté through a sieve or stir it with a fork and add some extra cream which you have mixed with a little salt, herbs, port and the like.

An extra spicy jelly, made just fluid and stirred into the mixture, also works very well. Or make cubes of salt meat and/or jelly and stir them through the pâté. Do not serve a bland pâté too cold, this makes it even blander.

A pâté which is too spicy or too salty

You did not taste it often enough, or you did not taste carefully enough. If it is not too bad, stirring in a little plain jelly or unsalted butter or cream, and serving it cold, will be enough. If not, you should fry some chicken livers or another kind of liver, purée them and, with a little fat (bacon fat, cream or butter) or jelly, mix this into the pâté. Or mash everything up and, with some extra fat or jelly, mix in cubes of unsalted, cooked meat, game, poultry or liver.

Pâté which you think is unsuitable to serve as a lunch dish, or as a starter, or as a main dish, is excellent as a filling for something else: stuff onions, artichokes, mushrooms, tomatoes, aubergines, peppers, cabbage or another vegetable with the pâté and gratin them in the oven. Or make vegetable rolls. Use a thick slice of raw meat (pork fillet or something), cut it diagonally, so you get a small envelope and fill with the pâté. Sew the pieces together and fry the meat.

Make a stuffed chicken, pigeon or other bird, with pâté. Put a layer of pâté on a pastry crust, pour over an egg-cream mixture, as described under egg and cheese flans and bake the flan.

If your pâté was successful and very nice, but did not go down too well either with your or your guests, then stick to the excellent medical advice from a medieval cookery book: *A boisterous laugh is an approved remedy for indigestion and other complaints after a meal.*

INDEX